FOOD LOVERS'
GUIDE TO
CHARLOTTE

The Best Restaurants, Markets & Local Culinary Offerings

1st Edition

Sarah Crosland

gpp

Guilford, Connecticut

Editor: Kevin Sirois
Project Editor: Julie Marsh
Layout Artist: Mary Ballachino
Text Design: Sheryl Kober
Illustrations by Jill Butler with additional art by Carleen Moira Powell and MaryAnn Dubé
Maps: Alena Joy Pearce © Morris Book Publishing, LLC

ISBN 978-0-7627-8110-2

Printed in the United States of America
10 9 8 7 6 5 4 3 2

All the information in this guidebook is subject to change. We recommend that you call ahead
to obtain current information before traveling.

Contents

About the Author

Sarah Crosland grew up in a small North Carolina town outside of Charlotte where she developed an appreciation for the region's homegrown veggies, excellent barbecue, and addictive sweet tea. As a kid, her first tastes of upscale dining came from special-occasion visits to the city's steakhouses and bistros with her family.

Fast forward a few years and Sarah has had the opportunity to travel around the world, enjoying renowned restaurants run by world-famous chefs—and digging into meals served from street vendors and prepared in local homes. She has developed a love of international flavors—and the cultures behind them.

After covering food and dining as an editor for *The Atlantan* magazine in Atlanta, Georgia, Sarah returned in 2008 to her home state to cover Charlotte's growing culinary scene as the dining editor for *Charlotte* magazine. While working at the magazine, Sarah reviewed countless local restaurants, launched and authored the magazine's food-and-beverage blog, authored the annual "Charlotte's Best Restaurants" feature, and judged local culinary contests.

Sarah enjoys checking out the city's latest see-and-be-seen spots, but her real passion lies in finding the restaurants, chefs, and dishes that offer a true taste of Charlotte. An avid locavore, Sarah has spent many weekends visiting area farms and markets to get a glimpse of the city's dining scene quite literally from farm to fork. And as someone who grew up on a farm just down the road, she loves to learn and share the stories behind the local fare you're eating.

Acknowledgments

First, I have to thank my wonderful parents and brother who have always made me believe I can do anything—even write a book. I also want to thank my friends Blake, Christy, Emily, Jenn, Joanna, and Katie for coming with me to try countless meals—and always letting me eat off your plate.

I couldn't have written this book without all of the knowledge of Charlotte restaurants generously imparted to me by *Charlotte* magazine's editor-in-chief, Rick Thurmond. His years of covering the city and its dining scene gave me context for the story of every restaurant.

And finally, I want to thank my editor Kevin Sirois and Globe Pequot Press for giving me this incredible opportunity to highlight my favorite city and its amazing culinary scene. I'm grateful for the experience.

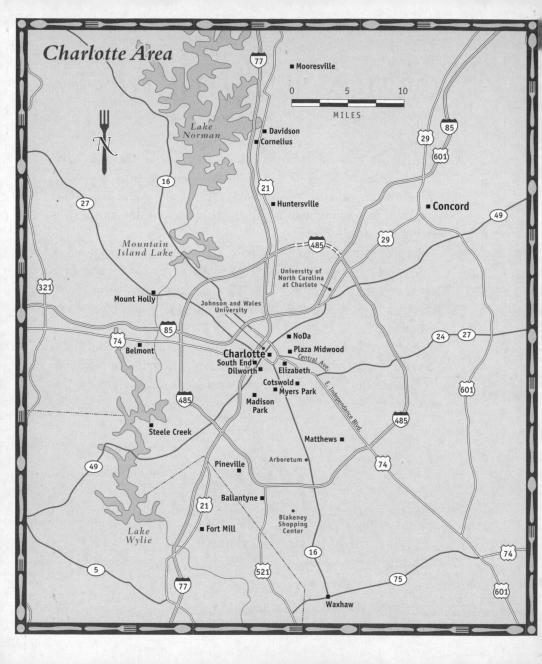

Introduction

Charlotte: New South Dining

Charlotte isn't your typically southern city. Sure, there are the oak-lined drives in Myers Park and the historic mills in South End. But with its gleaming skyscrapers filled with Fortune 500 companies and popular public transit system, Charlotte has a diverse and urbane vibe that you won't find in many other spots around the South.

And it's not just Charlotte's appearance that gives it this feeling. Meeting a native Charlottean can seem like a rare occurrence in this city that is the second-largest banking headquarters in the nation behind New York. In the last several decades international businesses—particularly banking—have drawn people from around the country and the world to make their home in the Queen City.

While the growth at first came in the form of luxury housing developments and more of those skyscrapers, these days the city's vibrant cultural scene is best seen in its small neighborhoods and locally owned restaurants and businesses. And Charlotte's culinary scene has quickly caught up to its financial boom with locals embracing trends like food trucks and farm-to-fork, as well as soaking up the new flavors brought by international transplants to the region.

Just a few years ago, your culinary choices for a weekend in Charlotte may have been limited to steakhouse fare and some soul food if you could track it down. Now, you can eat Southern favorite biscuits and gravy made with local sausage for breakfast, chew through a traditional Vietnamese *banh mi* for lunch, spend the afternoon shopping in a local farmers' market, and scoop up your dinner with your hands at an Ethiopian spot for dinner. From sexy sushi lounges to down-home country kitchens, there's no shortage of options for any taste. And, of course, there are still plenty of those award-winning steakhouses where you're likely to spot a local bigwig while you dig into a juicy—and often locally raised—cut of beef.

But don't just spend a weekend in Charlotte. This is a spot where you'll want to stay for awhile. After all, its booming business and international appeal may make it the New South, but this is still a southern city where time moves a little slower, especially when it comes to lingering over your favorite dishes. So bring your sense of adventure and settle in because whether you're eating buttermilk fried chicken or chicken *chettinadu* curry, Charlotte's culinary scene offers much to savor.

How to Use This Book

This book is separated into different neighborhoods and areas of Charlotte and its surrounding region. Within each you'll find these helpful features.

Foodie Faves

These restaurants are each worth a visit (or two) and include everything from cozy neighborhood diners full of local families to the spots where you'll find the hottest chef in town creating innovative dishes for stylish crowds.

Landmarks

These are restaurants that are more institutions than actual dining locales. Their food can range from decent to delicious, but half the time, it's barely even the point. The point is that these places are iconic destinations with enough character to compensate for any small flaws.

Specialty Stores, Markets & Producers

Home to Johnson & Wales culinary school, many small cooking classes, and plenty of Southerners who grew up with an appreciation for skills in the kitchen, Charlotte has more than its fair share of aspiring chefs. These shops are perfect for picking up prepared dishes or finding just the right ingredients for your next gourmet meal.

Recipes

Many of the dishes mentioned in these pages are the kinds you can't get out of your head. (We're looking at you, Salted-Caramel Brownies from Amelie's French Bakery.) Luckily, we've included their recipes in the back of this book, which means you can make them any time you want—which will likely be often.

Price Code

Whether you're searching for $2 tacos or in the mood for a luxurious multicourse dinner, Charlotte offers a price point for any eater. We've included the following scale system based on the average price of a single entree:

$	Less than $10
$$	$10 to $20
$$$	More than $20

Festivals & Events

With its brisk winters and warm, breezy summers, Charlotte is a city that loves to enjoy the outdoors. This means that many of the city's dining events can be found under tents in parks and along city sidewalks on sunny days. A lot of the city's festivals focus on two North Carolina favorites—NASCAR and barbecue. But when it comes to food festivities, there's something for every taste, from elegant wine tastings in an upscale setting to stacks of sticky baklava at a bustling Greek festival. Those in search of a taste of Charlotte don't have to look far.

January & July

Charlotte Restaurant Week, charlotterestaurantweek.com. There is no better time than this biannual, weeklong event to try out the city's top restaurants. Not only does Restaurant Week offer the chance to dine for just $30 a person at more than 100 different area restaurants, but it also means that diners can get a taste of some of the restaurant's top offerings from each course. If you're trying to get a bargain at high-priced spots like **BLT Steak** (p. 25) or **Del Frisco's** (p. 148), make your reservations early because the secret is out when it comes to these upscale restaurants. And while you will find excellent offerings there, some of the best meals are from smaller spots like **Carpe Diem** (p. 144) in Elizabeth, which always offers its famed warm goat cheese salad and grilled duck breast, or **Passion8 Bistro** (p. 206), where seasonal dishes mean that each of your choices is fresh and locally sourced.

March

Charlotte Beer Week, charlottecraftbeerweek.org. Charlotte's beer scene is growing rapidly and nowhere is that more evident than with this annual week dedicated to all things beer. Local restaurants and pubs that are favorites of Charlotte beer nerds offer events all week long, including keg tapping, beer dinners, tastings, and even beer brunches. If you prefer your beer with a side of something tasty, make plans to attend events at places like **Pizza Peel** (p. 164), where you'll get locally brewed beers paired with artisan pizza pies, or **Mac's Speed Shop** (p. 69), where your pint comes alongside a heaping plate of barbecue. However, you'll find hearty fare paired with regional brews at almost all of the events and it's hard to beat the scenery for ones like that at the US National Whitewater Center, where you can enjoy your cold one next to the rapids.

April

Charlotte Wine & Food Weekend, charlottewineandfood.org. This swanky weekend raises thousands of dollars for local charities, which means you can feel good while you're sipping away. The weekend's events are in locations around Charlotte and most have a decidedly upscale feel with tastings hosted by top sommeliers and vintner dinners held in some of the area's most sophisticated restaurants. One of the most popular events—and the largest of the weekend—is the annual Big Bottles & Blues. It offers the chance to sample all of the winery guests from the weekend while you enjoy live music and local cuisine (think barbecue and mac and cheese). Plus, guests can bid on wine bottles and wine dinners at the live and silent auctions, giving you the chance to continue enjoying the region's wine and food long after the weekend.

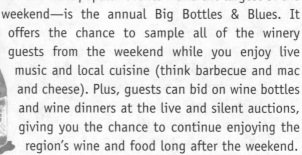

NASCAR Noshing

If there's anyone who knows how to indulge in good food and good times, it's NASCAR fans. So, it should come as no surprise that events based around the races tend to have some of the most fun fare around. The granddaddy of the race-related festivals is **Food Lion Speed Street,** the annual uptown event based around the May races at Charlotte Motor Speedway. With a large stage in the center of the city, the event includes plenty of live entertainment from national acts and family-friendly events. You'll also find just about any kind of street festival food you care to enjoy, from burgers and dogs to funnel cakes and fries.

But you'll have to go to the track itself to get some of the most creative fair foods. For events like the Food Lion AutoFair, the NASCAR Sprint All-Star Race, and the Coca-Cola 600, Levy Restaurants creates dishes like deep-fried peaches, pimento mac and cheese balls mixed with bacon and deep fried, and bologna-q sandwiches made with deep-fried strips of bologna and barbecue sauce. Or, if you're there early enough, you can dig into dishes like the breakfast sundae, offering layers of biscuits, eggs, sausage, gravy, grits, and cheese. Levy creates new Southern-inspired dishes each year, so keep an eye on the Speedway's website (charlottemotorspeedway.com) to see what's cooking for the next NASCAR event.

May

Beer, Bourbon & BBQ Festival, beerandbourbon.com. Sure, you could go to this traveling festival in places like Atlanta or Nashville, but you're unlikely to find a better spot than Charlotte for digging into local barbecue while you sample more than 60 beers and more than 40 bourbons. Grab a plate of ribs, brisket, or even just a chopped sandwich, get your souvenir glass filled from your favorite local brewery, and then head down to the SouthPark waterside where you can sit in the grass and watch live music on The Main Stage. While kids 12 and under can get in for free, this event tends to get a little rowdy as the day goes on (did you see that part about more than 40 bourbons?), so bring your 21 and up friends for this festival.

June

Taste of Charlotte, tasteofcharlotte.com. Yes, it's hot—after all, it's summer in the South. And yes, it gets crowded, especially during lunch hour on Friday when seemingly every uptown worker hits Tryon Street in search of a bite. But don't let either of these things deter you from this massive uptown street festival featuring tastes from some of the city's best restaurants, live music, and entertainment. Taste of Charlotte works on a coin system such that you purchase coins, which you then give to the restaurant booths in exchange for their food. There are generally some chain restaurants included, but the majority of the restaurants are smaller, locally owned spots offering a taste of their fare with food ranging from cupcakes from a local bake shop to pork sliders from an uptown restaurant.

September

Oktoberfest, charlotteoktoberfest.com. This festival is crowded, often quite hot, and held in a field that often requires waiting in lines of traffic to enter. In other words, if you don't really love beer, this may not be the one for you. However, if you're fond of your brews—or if you just enjoy what is essentially a giant outdoor party—you've come to the right place. This annual event features breweries from around the world, with many coming from the southeast. Ticket holders get a souvenir glass when they enter and then it's up to you just how many of the more than 350 beers you can handle sampling. Ready for a break from the brews? There's a stage with live music and food vendors, including **Mac's Speed Shop** (p. 69), offering bites to enjoy alongside your beer.

Time Warner Cable BBQ & Blues, charlottebbqand blues.com. If you're a fan of barbecue, there's no better spot in Charlotte than this festival for getting your fill of it. The hardest part of the event is actually choosing which 'cue vendor you want to try. You'll find plates of ribs, chopped sandwiches, and slabs of pork, all alongside traditional sides like baked beans, grilled corn, potato salad, and coleslaw. Sure, there are other offerings like hot dogs, fries, funnel cakes, and even Greek foods, but this event is dedicated to all things barbecue. So grab a plate of it and settle in for national blues acts like Buddy Guy or Jimmie Vaughan. Oh, and before you leave, grab a fresh apple slushie from Mercier Orchards. This event kicks off the Charlotte fall season and the slushies are the perfect sweet fall flavor for ending the night.

Yiasou Greek Festival, yiasoufestival.org. The annual festival has been going on for more than 30 years. Held in the historic Dilworth neighborhood at the Holy Trinity Greek Orthodox Cathedral, the family-friendly event offers a taste of Greek culture—quite literally. You can go on tours of the gorgeous church, catch live traditional Greek entertainment, and even shop in an outdoor craft market, but the main reason to come to this popular festival is the tasty fare. Here you'll find Grecian baked chicken, gyro and souvlaki sandwiches, spanakopitas, Greek salads, Athenian baked fish, kalamata olives, Greek cheeses, and even Greek wines. Whatever you order, don't skip the baklava. Drenched in honey, these sweet, delicate pastries are worth the sticky fingers and extra calories. Just interested in the food? The event offers a drive-through menu, which means you can pull up and grab a dinner plate and assorted pastries to go.

Keeping Up with Food News

Charlotte's dining scene is ever-evolving, and like many cities, there's almost always an interesting story behind every dish, restaurant opening, and chef move. If you're interested in finding news on the latest and greatest, or hoping for information on your favorite restaurant or chef, these local publications, websites, blogs, and Twitter accounts offer the best insight into and advice on the city's culinary happenings.

Charlotte Food Bloggers, charlottefoodbloggers.wordpress.com. This group of local food bloggers meets monthly to chat about all things food and blogging. While a bloggers' blog may not be helpful, the links to the members' blogs will direct you to lots of local foodies. Many of the blogs are primarily focused on cooking and geared toward a national audience, but you'll also find local bloggers covering the city's dining scene from niches like vegan eating and strictly baking.

Charlotte **magazine's Dine & Dish Blog,** charlottemagazine .com/blogs/dine-dish. You'll find this blog on the home page of the city magazine, *Charlotte* magazine. The magazine itself offers restaurant reviews, chef interviews, and food features like its annual "Best Restaurants" package. But on the blog you'll find up-to-the-minute information on upcoming food events, new restaurants, and dining news.

***Charlotte Observer's* Helen Schwab,** helendining.blogspot .com. Helen Schwab is one of the city's best-known dining critics and readers can find her reviews and restaurant news in the pages of the daily newspaper, the *Charlotte Observer.* Her blog features breaking news about the restaurant scene as well as first looks at new spots. And if you're looking for dining specials on holidays like Thanksgiving, Christmas, or Valentine's Day, there's no better blog in town to find them all in one place.

Charlotte's Got a Lot, charlottes gotalot.com. The city's travel and tourism site is dedicated to sharing its best restaurants with visitors and locals alike, so you'll find updated informa- tion on its restaurants, bakeries, bars, coffee shops, delis, and more on this site. Just select the kind of food you're in the mood for and pick your location, and it offers a comprehensive list of where to eat.

CLT Dining, cltdining.com; @cltdining. Craig Utt, this site's owner, frequently updates the site with information about dining specials and new restaurants. However, for the real up-to-the- minute deals, check out his Twitter feed, where he frequently tweets special offers from local restaurants and re-tweets top restaurant-related information, photos, and deals.

Creative Loafing's Eat My Charlotte, clclt.com/blogs/eatmy charlotte. This blog is a combination of restaurant and bar news and reviews, as well as a guide to cooking in the Queen City. This means that in addition to finding helpful information about local eateries, you'll also get plenty of information on food shops, breweries, and wine stores around town as well as tips from local chefs and bartenders on how to create their favorites.

WFAEats, wfaeats.org. Published by 90.7 WFAE, Charlotte's NPR News Source, this entertaining blog offers food stories and recipes, as well as updates on city food events. It also directs you to when you can listen in on 90.7 for interviews with local chefs, Johnson & Wales professors, and restaurant owners when they give their takes on the city's food scene.

Food Trucks

The national food truck trend has taken off in Charlotte, where you'll find the trucks around town almost every day. These colorful trucks offer everything from sweet cupcakes on the run to gourmet pork tacos made with locally raised and grown meat and veggies. Tracking down the truck of your choice can be a little tricky, but keep an eye on its website or Twitter feed and you're likely to find that they're serving somewhere close by.

Clover Joe's Sandwich Shoppe, (803) 631-3501; facebook
.com/clover.joes. This truck is actually based out of Clover, South
Carolina—hence the name—but you'll find it around Charlotte each
week, often making the rounds in South End on Camden Road. Just
look for the white truck with the green lettering and a chalkboard
menu. The menu offers tasty sandwich combos like chicken Caesar
subs, BLTs, and cheeseburgers, which all come with a drink and
chips. And for those looking on the lighter side, Clover Joe's has
also added salads to its menu. Ready for a cheesesteak break? Check
out Clover Joe's Facebook page for the most up-to-date information
on where you can find the truck.

Cupcake Delirium, (704) 458-9389; cupcakedelirium.com; @
onthegocupcakes. These aren't just your typical cupcakes. This
baby-blue truck serves up cakes like The Earl of Swirls, an Earl Grey–
scented cupcake with lemon curd filling and vanilla buttercream

or the Mountain Dew Cupcake featuring a
Mountain Dew–flavored cake with green
Mountain Dew frosting. And while you
can frequently find the truck cruising the
streets in Plaza Midwood and Uptown,
if you need your cupcake fix fast, Cupcake Delirium offers free
deliveries for one dozen cupcakes of the same flavor. Trying
to decide which one to indulge in 12 times over? Consider the
S'more Cupcake, a moist chocolate cupcake topped with chocolate
ganache, toasted marshmallows, and crumbled graham crackers.
Campfire not included.

Harvest Moon Grille, (828) 234-5182; ggfarm.com; @HMGCart. When the women behind the local Grateful Growers Farm launched this food truck, it was the first high-quality truck in town. Offering all locally grown or raised fare, the bright orange truck was an instant success—so much so, in fact, that they've since launched a restaurant under the same name. While the orange truck was unfortunately stolen, a shiny navy blue version has replaced it and continues to serve up the same fresh food, much of it straight from Grateful Growers Farm. Here you'll typically find three daily options with one generally being vegetarian like a falafel with chowchow aioli, and at least one being pork focused such as a pork burger topped with sautéed peppers and onions. Look for the truck at the corner of Trade and Tryon on warmer days, but if you can't find it, you can always head down to the brick-and-mortar business at 235 North Tryon.

Holy Matrimony Wingzza Truck, (704) 737-1040; wingzzatruck .com; @WingzzaTruck. With a black truck that looks more like it should have motorcycles in the back than any food, this casual food truck is serving up pizza and wings roadside. Don't come here searching for health foods—this one is strictly to satisfy your cravings for cheesy pizzas and finger-licking wings. You'll find them all around Uptown Charlotte and frequently in the University area. Feeling seriously hungry? Wingzza offers wings orders up to 100 wings ($69.99).

Chow Down Uptown

This food truck festival, which started in May 2011, has become an instant favorite among Queen City foodies—and with good reason. The event, which happens on various Thursday evenings at locations around Charlotte, offers the chance to sample from a variety of the city's top trucks. The trucks all gather in one location such as uptown on 7th St. across from the new City Market or in South End at Atherton Mill.

The event used to be strictly just food trucks serving their fare, but these days it has expanded to wine and beer tastings, and entertainment ranging from string bands to slam poets. But the focus is still on the food with many of the local favorite trucks showing up to serve their most popular dishes. Whether you're a food-truck fanatic, or ready to sample curbside fare for the first time, this is a fun way to taste what Charlotte's food truck scene has to offer. For more info, check out facebook.com/ChowDownUptown or e-mail chowdownuptown@gmail.com.

Maki Taco, (704) 380-0381; makitaco.com; @makitacotruck. This is a truck offering inexpensive, gourmet pan-Asian tacos. As in, tacos like a chicken soft taco with a panang curry sauce or a crispy shrimp taco with a teriyaki sauce, all with toppings like red peppers, cucumbers, peanuts, or scallions. The food is fresh, local, and all-natural and there are plenty of vegetarian options. Basically, there is absolutely no reason for you to still be reading this and not out tracking down these tacos. You can find them on Saturday at Atherton Market in South End; otherwise check their Twitter feed for their latest location.

Napolitanos, (704) 989-3254; napolitanositalian market.com; @NapolitanosMkt. It's hard to miss this food truck—it's the one covered in bright red tomatoes. This family-owned business serves up homemade sausages and classic Italian dishes like fried eggplant heroes or meatball subs. Craving a New York City–style street food fix? Napolitanos has you covered with all-beef hotdogs served with warm sauerkraut and spicy onion relish or Jewish dumplings stuffed with savory potato filling and deep fried. The mix may seem strange, but the family behind the business is from Italy via Brooklyn so you're getting an authentic taste of both spots.

Outdoor Feasts, (803) 487-6876; outdoorfeasts.com; @danpigman. The guy with the Southern drawl behind the window of this truck goes by Dan the Pig Man and as you might imagine, he is pretty serious about his pork. Dan Huntley runs a catering business out of Rock Hill and the Lake Wylie area, but you'll frequently find him on the streets and at events around Charlotte selling his local fare. More complex dishes like a Boudin French sausage with rice make the menu, but you'll want to order something that comes with his award-winning Carolina Pig Pucker BBQ Sauce. It's a family recipe for a tangy Carolina sauce and when served over ribs or chicken is lip-smacking good. Just ask for extra napkins.

Roaming Fork, (321) 229-1485; roamingfork.net. There are plenty of tasty choices on the menu of this bright green truck, but if you don't order the fried pimento cheesy balls, you're really doing yourself a disservice. They won't be winning any health-food awards, but these creamy fried bites are just as decadent and delicious as you might imagine. The truck's main dishes are sandwiches, but not of your average variety, with amusingly named options like Not Your Mama's Meatloaf on crunchy sour-dough bread or Ooey Gooey Grilled Cheese, featuring pulled pork and barbecue sauce. Ready for those pimento cheese balls yet? The truck's website includes a monthly calendar showing its neighbor-hood locations.

Roots Farm Food Truck, (301) 471-1366; rootsfarmfood.com. This cart is serious about its farm-to-fork dishes, or as they call it, "soil to soul." With a Johnson & Wales grad in the kitchen, the food here is sourced from farms that are less than 100 miles away. Dishes are seasonal and organically inspired with choices like a spinach salad with pickled ginger and green onion, with a honey miso dressing, or a toasted-turkey-with-brie-and-apples sandwich. You'll find the truck at just about any food-truck gig around town and you can always check the website for up-to-the-minute updates on its roving location.

Smoke n Go, (704) 819-7606; smokeandgoclt.com; @smokengo cafe. This Huntersville-based truck comes with a 16-foot smoker and walking by it without salivating offers a serious challenge. Slow-cooked ribs, chicken, beef briskets, and turkey legs are served fall-off-the-bone-tender and with a classic smokey flavor. You'll also find sides like potato salad and coleslaw. And while it may be tempting after a plateful of this food, whatever you do, don't skip dessert. The homemade banana pudding is the perfect creamy finish to a Carolina curbside meal.

Southern Cake Queen, (704) 287-8314; southerncakequeen .com; @southerncake. Emma Merisier, the owner, driver, and pastry chef behind this giant pink truck may be the sweetest thing inside of it. And that's saying a lot considering the former UPS truck is stocked with some of the town's tastiest cupcakes. Merisier dishes out creative cupcakes in flavors like lemon drop, Key lime coconut, and even egg nog. But try to plan your cupcake order here around strawberry season when you'll find the Signature Strawberry cupcake made with fresh pureed strawberries and topped with pink vanilla buttercream. Merisier calls it her favorite for a good reason.

Uptown Charlotte

Spend an evening in Uptown Charlotte and you'll be hitting the streets among theatergoers, bar-crawlers, and concert-watchers. The city's after-dark scene is thriving with a new nightlife complex and even newer arts center now among its skyscrapers. Wide sidewalks fill up in the evenings with locals and visitors out to dinner or drinks at one of Uptown's many restaurants.

But it wasn't always this way. For decades, Charlotte was strictly a weekday city with bankers and businessmen heading home to the 'burbs as soon as the day's work was complete. Urban planners and real estate developers worked together, though, adding lofts, apartments, and hotels to the city center, as well as restaurants, bars, and lounges. And while a little more than 10 years ago, Uptown was no man's land on weekend nights, today it offers a vibrant dining and nightlife scene. In fact, the only time when uptown's streets are busier than a Saturday night may be during weekday lunch hour when workers spill out of the new buildings and into restaurants and sandwich shops for a quick, midday bite.

Split into four historic wards at the central intersection of Trade and Tryon Streets, Uptown offers everything from quaint Victorian homes on tree-shaded streets to gleaming skyscrapers housing international corporations. And its dining options reflect that diversity. Here you'll find a cozy neighborhood pub just a few blocks from a sleek sushi restaurant. And while swanky steakhouses have long reigned on the city's dining scene, these days you're just as likely to see crowds lining up at organic food trucks parked on city squares.

And don't even think about calling Charlotte's city center Downtown—it's always Uptown. Rumors abound as to why exactly this is the case. Many locals will tell you that it has always been called Uptown because the intersection of Trade and Tryon is the highest point of elevation in the area. But others attest that the word Downtown was used until the 1980s when the city began to try to promote a more positive image of itself and switched to the more upbeat Uptown.

Regardless of how it was named, Uptown definitely has a positive vibe these days. But don't take my word for it—head to one of these top restaurants and experience what it offers for yourself.

Foodie Faves

Amelie's French Bakery, 330 S. Tryon St., Charlotte, NC 28205; (704) 376-1782; ameliesfrenchbakery.com; Bakery/French; $. This is the second location of this immensely popular French bakery. At the original spot (p. 95), just a few minutes across town, you'll find crowds filling the overstuffed couches and bistro tables 24 hours a day. This miniature satellite version isn't quite as eclectic—or as constantly packed—as its charming sister, but you'll still find the same delicious fare and strong coffee. Mornings find local workers stopping in for their gourmet lattes and at lunchtime a line often winds to the door with orders for soups and sandwiches. However, the best time for enjoying the comfy cafe is when you have time to relax with a warm drink and one of their famed salted caramel brownies. With this sweet dessert, featuring a dense brownie topped with smooth, salty caramel, you'll likely start craving your next before you've finished your first. See Owner Lynn St. Laurent and Assistant Pastry Chef Eric Stanton's recipe for **Salted-Caramel Brownies** on p. 256.

Aria Tuscan Grill, 100 N. Tryon St., Charlotte, NC 28202; (704) 376-8880; ariacharlotte.com; Italian; $$$. A sleek and chic creation from local restaurateur Pierre Bader, this Italian restaurant has become the city's place to see and be seen. Inside the glass doors you'll find an often-crowded bar area with the young and stylish mingling over cocktails until late into the evening. The contemporary dining room offers views into the kitchen, but the best seat in the house is at the Chef's Table, an elegant private dining area for up to eight, just off the kitchen. The Tuscan dishes here are excellent with hearty portions of handmade pasta and rich sauces. And you won't want to skip appetizers or desserts. The caramelized gnocchi appetizer featuring airy pillows of gnocchi tossed in a pear, Gorgonzola cream, and truffle sauce is the menu's star, while a lemon *semifreddo* dessert offers the perfect cold, sweet finish to an evening.

Basil Thai, 210 N. Church St., Charlotte, NC 28202; (704) 332-7212; eatatbasil.com; Thai; $$$. Prior to the arrival of this chic restaurant, your best bet for Thai food in Charlotte could be found in strip malls and small settings. But that changed when brothers Henry and Chai Eang brought their Charleston, South Carolina, concept to the Queen City. This trendy spot features dramatic street views and sexy decor with a floor-to-ceiling red velvet curtain accenting the dining area. The menu offers traditional Thai fare expertly created using fresh ingredients. Curry options offer a spicy kick, but the pad thai with its delicate rice noodles and tender chicken and shrimp is a tasty variation of this traditional Thai street food. A mango and sticky rice dessert made with fresh slices of the sweet fruit, is the perfect ending to an evening indulging in some of South Asia's favorite fare. Don't forget to make reservations here on the weekends when the dining room and small bar fill up quickly.

Bask on Seaboard, 1000 Seaboard St., Charlotte, NC 28206; (980) 613-8282; baskonseaboard.com; Lounge, American; $$. If you're looking for a swanky meal alongside your entertainment experience, this spot located in the North Carolina Music Factory is your place. Dark hardwood floors, exposed brick walls, and white leather accents make up the interior of the sleek restaurant where you'll find entrees like filet mignon in a Coca-Cola demi-glace. The nature of the restaurant and its patio encourages lingering after a show or enjoying a few drinks and appetizers before heading over to one of the popular nightclubs on the premises. You'll find several local beers and more than 30 wines by the glass, but you'll want to try cocktails like the Champagne julep made with Cava, bourbon, mint, and simple syrup. Looking for an appetizer to share with the table? Dig in to the scotch Eggs rolled in local sausage and deep fried before being served atop soft herb cheese.

Bentley's on 27, 201 S. College St., 27th Flr., Charlotte, NC 28244; (704) 343-9201; bentleyson27.com; French; $$$. While the menu is impressive, it's hard for anything to top the skyline views from this 27th-floor restaurant. Request a window table and schedule dinner during sunset, then let the skilled sommelier direct you on wine choices. Steak dishes dominate the entrees, while appetizers show off some of the kitchen's best skills with seafood with a decadent macaroni and cheese featuring lobster and truffles, and a tuna carpaccio perfectly paired with a soy mustard butter sauce. While dinner is prime time with its twilight views, the restaurant is open for lunch as well and is one spot you're certain to make an impression. The menu is similar to dinner, but does offer a selection of sandwiches including a particularly tasty prime rib sandwich topped with mozzarella, arugula, and sliced tomato, and slathered in a creamy basil aioli. It's not the dinner's tender steaks, but for a midday meal, it's an excellent sub.

Bernardin's Restaurant, 435 S. Tryon St., Charlotte, NC 28202; (704) 332-3188; bernardinsfinedining.com; Asian/French; $$$. This is a favorite of museum visitors and those headed to shows at the Levine Center for the Arts across the street. Housed in a historic florist's shop, the charming dining area features arched ceilings and white lights strung between the walls. It's the second location of the restaurant with the original being in Winston-Salem, but its cozy dining area and well-executed dishes make it feel like an original. While the menu is mostly contemporary American, you'll find Asian and French influences as well, such as a tuna appetizer featuring three different preparations of fresh ahi tuna. For adventurous eaters, there are a few items you're unlikely to find on many Charlotte menus, such as grilled New Zealand venison, pan-seared ostrich, or a free-range bison strip loin served with bone marrow truffle butter. It's the kind of global cuisine that's often hard to find in this era of locavore love.

BLT Steak, 110 N. College St., Charlotte, NC 28202; (704) 972-4381; e2hospitality.com; Steakhouse; $$$. This international chain, named after its original chef (Bistro Laurent Tourendel), added some serious style to Uptown when it arrived. Housed in the bottom floor of the eco-friendly Ritz-Carlton and new Bank of America tower, the restaurant is the city's latest and greatest steakhouse.

It's known for its steaks for a reason and you won't go wrong with a filet or rib eye, but a la carte sides like jalapeño mashed potatoes and seared Brussels sprouts are tasty as well. Of course, the best part of the meal may be the crusty gruyère popovers, offered complimentary and served hot at each table. Not in the mood for a full dinner, but want to check out the scene? BLT's cocktails are some of the best—and most creative—in town. Grab a seat at the bar and try the Rosemary Margarita.

Blue Restaurant & Bar, 214 N. Tryon St., Charlotte, NC 28202; (704) 927-2583; bluecharlotte.com; Mediterranean; $$$. This longtime Charlotte favorite is known for two things: the city's best upscale Mediterranean fare and a martini list that will make your mouth water (think crème brûlée, caramel flan, cookies and cream, and chocolate mousse). If you're there early in the evening, you're likely to see Uptown workers mingling over the famed martinis and appetizers, while later the restaurant offers live jazz music and an appetizing bar menu. But go during the dinner hour when you can try dishes like Chef Gene Briggs's simmering lamb tagine, a savory Moroccan dish with slow-roasted lamb shank. Enjoy what you ate? Chef Briggs offers frequent cooking classes revealing the full process of complex dishes like beef bourguignon. The classes are themed by region, style, and dish, which means you might find a "Picnic in the South of France" class in midsummer and an "Autumn Game Dishes" class in early fall.

The Burger Co., 1500 W. Morehead St., Ste. C, Westside, Charlotte, NC 28208; (704) 332-7333; theburgercompany.com; Hamburgers; $. Located in the area just off Uptown known to locals as the Westside, this burger joint is the kind of place where you can expect to enjoy loud music, salty fries, and a cold beer alongside a burger you'll definitely need two hands and plenty of napkins to eat. It fills up fast during the weekday lunch hour with those craving one of its juicy cheeseburgers and sweet potato fries. While you could go the route of creating your own burger, some of the best options are under the stuffed burgers—beef patties stuffed with cheddar cheese. For an excuse to enjoy an extra one of the restaurant's cold beers, try the Firehouse Burger topped with spicy aioli, chili, and jalapeños.

The Capital Grille, 201 N. Tryon St., Charlotte, NC 28202; (704) 348-1400; thecapitalgrille.com; Steakhouse; $$$. The private dining rooms of this restaurant have seen many of Charlotte's biggest banking deals. The Capital Grille has been around for longer than many of the local steakhouses and there are plenty of locals who continue to swear by it. Located in the center of Uptown, the elegant steakhouse features paintings of local figures on the walls, white tablecloths, and impeccable service. The steaks and seafood are prepared well and of the standard you'd expect from this renowned chain. One of the top sellers, though, is the calamari, featuring the tender fried fish alongside olives with a cool sauce for dipping. You're unlikely to see a table not enjoying a heaping plate of the dish most nights. Other top choices include the lobster mac and cheese, shrimp cocktail, and a cheesecake dessert with a caramelized top covered in berries and freshly whipped cream.

Chima Brazilian Steakhouse, 139 S. Tryon St., Charlotte, NC 28202; (980) 225-5000; chima.cc; Brazilian; $$$. You're going to want to loosen your belt—and possibly skip a meal—before heading to this Brazilian steakhouse chain. The fixed-price menu includes a spectacular salad bar, unlimited a la carte sides, and more meat than any person should ever eat. In fact, you'll even find meat on the "salad" bar, which includes dishes like a flavorful beef carpaccio, calamari salad, and slices of prosciutto, as well as arugula salad, gorgonzola cheese mousse, and fresh cheeses. Servers, wearing traditional Brazilian garb complete with gaucho pants, will cut your choice of meat for you, from chicken and pork to steak and lamb, until you've had your fill. While you'll likely be too full to move following a meal here, the upstairs bar, which often features live music, is one of the city's best spots to relax with a late-evening drink.

Dandelion Market, 118 W. 5th St., Charlotte, NC 28202; (704) 333-7989; dandelionmarketcharlotte.com; American/Irish; $. If you're going strictly for food, don't show up after 10 p.m. because on the weekends this local pub turns into one of the city's hottest nightspots. However, during lunch, dinner, and Sunday brunch, you'll find sandwiches and savory small plates. Lunchtime fills the downstairs dining room with Uptown workers digging into one of the spot's stuffed sandwiches or tasty salads. At dinner, the prosciutto crostini featuring crisp crostinis topped with fresh prosciutto, sweet fig preserves, and caramelized onions is a favorite, and plan on splitting an order of the house *pomme frites* in order to enjoy the house-made ketchup (its recipe includes Guinness). Feeling hungry? The entire menu can be ordered—and hopefully shared—for $225.

Enso | Asian Bistro & Sushi Bar, 210 E. Trade St., Charlotte, NC 28202; (704) 716-3676; ensocharlotte.com; Asian/Sushi; $$. Located on the bottom floor of the EpiCentre nightlife complex, this sexy sushi bar is dimly lit, features plush decor, and plays thumping club beats late into the evening. While there's a full bistro menu with just about every common Asian dish imaginable (pad thai, curry, and sesame chicken to name a few), the best options on the menu are under sushi. The Bobcat Roll, named for the city's basketball team and featuring crab, salmon, and cucumber in a sweet Thai sauce, is a sure shot. Or, for a roll that should have a license to thrill, try the 007. It's cucumber, spicy tuna, and shrimp tempura all wrapped up and topped with crab, avocado, and spicy mayo.

E2 Emeril's Eatery, 135 Levine Avenue of the Arts, Charlotte, NC 28202; (704) 414-4787; e2emerils.com; Seafood/Southern; $$$.

Located in the stylish Levine Center for the Arts, this eatery is one of Charlotte's first tastes of the celebrity chef–driven restaurant. Owned by famed Cajun cuisine creator Emeril Lagasse, E2 offers a wide variety of foods ranging from burgers and salads to Emeril's classic Southern fare like shrimp and grits made with pancetta, tomato, and corn. Some of the menu's more creative options may be found at its raw bar. Indulge in adventurous dishes like a freshly shucked oyster shooter with pickled melon, parsley oil, and tomato water or yellowfin tuna tartare served with crisp taro chips. While the restaurant offers plenty of great seats, including tables with glimpses of the Mint Museum's large, changing screen, the best spot in the house is at the chef's bar, where you can get up close and personal with the chefs and watch as they prepare dishes like the warm huckleberry upside-down cake dessert. Served with brown-butter ice cream and salted caramel, you'll be tempted to be the one yelling "Bam!" when this plate hits your table.

Halcyon, Flavors from the Earth, 500 S. Tryon St., Charlotte, NC 28205; (704) 910-0865; halcyonflavors.com; American; $$$. Sure, the name seems a little over the top, but the carefully crafted dishes and drinks here more than live up to it. Located just off the entrance to the Mint Museum, Halcyon's floor-to-ceiling windows feature gorgeous views of Uptown's Green. A bar offers a glimpse into the kitchen where Chef Marc Jacksina works his magic, as well as a chance to order one of the creative drinks by the house mixologist such as the Some Pig, a mix of smoky Makers 46 steeped with bacon, orange bitters, and maple syrup. The menu changes seasonally and uses local ingredients. You'll never go wrong with the artisanal cheese board and freshly baked bread, and if the Phwah Burger, a house ground burger stuffed with foie gras and topped with egg and cheese, is on the menu, order it. Immediately. See Executive Chef Marc Jacksina's recipe for **Sweet Potato Crepes** on p. 250.

Harvest Moon Grille, 235 N. Tryon St., Charlotte, NC 28202; (704) 342-1193; harvestmoongrillecharlotte.com; American/Southern; $$. Cassie Parsons, the Chef and Owner behind this bright and simple restaurant off the lobby of the historic Dunhill Hotel, also happens to be the farmer who raises all of the pork you'll find on the menu. This means that whether you're ordering down-home biscuits and sausage gravy for breakfast, a modern *banh mi* for lunch, or an elegant pork tenderloin for dinner, the meat is the best you'll find in the city. Her farm, Grateful Growers, had been selling to local upscale restaurants for years before Parsons expanded to a food cart and then the restaurant. Everything on the menu is grown or raised within 100 miles of Charlotte and fresh, simple flavors shine through. The menu frequently changes, depending on seasonal produce, but cross your fingers you'll get lucky enough to be there when dishes like the pork belly braised in red wine and finished with a root beer reduction are on it.

The King's Kitchen, 129 W. Trade St., Charlotte, NC 28202; (704) 375-1990; kingskitchen.com; Southern; $$. While it may look like your typical, chic Uptown bistro, don't be deceived—there's nothing ordinary about this restaurant. The King's Kitchen is Owner and Chef Jim Noble's not-for-profit spot, which works with local businesses, ministries, and nonprofits to employ those in need of help and give money to local charities feeding the hungry. Don't think for a second that this gets in the way of this charitable restaurant turning out delicious fare. Noble's culinary talent shines in dishes like the veggie plates, "meat and threes," soups, salads, and sandwiches. Open for lunch and dinner, you'll find a down-home, Southern menu featuring options like deviled eggs, fried oysters, pork ribs, and even fried flounder. The most popular option—and with good and greasy reason—is Aunt Beaut's Skillet-Fried Chicken. Order it alongside fresh veggies like the butter beans, stewed tomatoes, and pan-seared cabbage for a meal that gives you as much as you're giving back.

LaVecchia's Steak & Seafood, 214 N. Tryon St., Charlotte, NC 28202; (704) 370-6776; lavecchias.com; Seafood/Steakhouse; $$$. Back in the days of the banking boom, this swanky seafood restaurant was the place to see and be seen. These days, things have settled down a bit and the restaurant has moved to a new location, but Nick LaVecchia's eatery remains one of the top spots in town to enjoy fresh Maine lobster, seared and plump jumbo scallops, or the signature lump crab cakes stuffed with tender white meat. And

GET SCHOOLED:
JOHNSON & WALES CHARLOTTE

When the famed school **Johnson & Wales** (801 W. Trade St., Charlotte, NC 28202; (980) 598-1000; jwu.edu/charlotte) opened their Charlotte campus in 1999, the culinary community rejoiced. Not only has the school brought in world-renowned chefs like Alice Waters or Thomas Keller to speak, but it quickly began producing culinary talent with an interest in the Queen City.

First, there were the chefs on faculty like Peter Reinhart, who is internationally known for his artisan pizzas and breads. Reinhart, who was previously in California, has now worked for more than a decade with chefs and restaurant owners around town developing their recipes and techniques.

But most exciting for Charlotte are the possibilities with each new class at JWU. These days, if you ask at any top local restaurant you're likely to find a JWU student in training on the wait staff or in the kitchen, if not a grad at the helm. And with new spots opening under the school's graduates, it seems likely that the city's culinary scene will only grow richer through it in coming years.

while the restaurant's Miami-meets-aquarium theme feels a little over-the-top these days, the patio just off the entrance to Hearst Tower is a perfect casual spot for a midday seafood wrap and fries or an evening cocktail alongside a plate of the oysters Rockefeller.

Luce, 214 N. Tryon St., Charlotte, NC 28202; (704) 344-9222; conte restaurantgroup.com; Italian; $$$. The host speaks with an Italian accent and the interior feels more Venetian than Charlottean, but the dishes here could speak for themselves. House-made pastas are served perfectly al dente and tossed in fragrant sauces like a traditional carbonara and a thick bolognese. Unexpectedly, one of the best times to visit the sophisticated Luce is during lunch when it's less crowded and the menu features smaller versions of the popular pastas, as well as crisp paninis stuffed with fresh cheeses and prosciutto. And while you may be tempted to skip the bread, knowing you have a rich pasta meal ahead, don't even think about it. The crusty, fresh loaves are served alongside flavorful olive oil and set the tone for the impressive meal. *Buon appetito!*

Malabar Spanish Cuisine, 214 N. Tryon St., Charlotte, NC 28202; (704) 344-8878; conterestaurantgroup.com; Spanish/Tapas; $$. In what used to be his upscale Italian spot, local restaurateur Augusto Conte opened this restaurant in 2012 dedicated to all things Spanish. The cozy interior includes views of Tryon Street, but for true Spanish cafe-style dining, snag a table on the restaurant's sidewalk patio—and order a carafe of the sweet sangria. Tapas options like ham, potato, and manchego *croquetas,* grilled octopus, eggplant bruschetta, and braised beef empanadas are all musts. But if you're in the mood for a heartier meal, order the paella. Be warned, it takes half an hour to get the freshly made traditional dish. But the *paella de pescado,* brimming with calamari, clams, mussels, shrimp, and cod, is worth the wait. Just make sure you choose your dining companion wisely—everything here, including the paella, is made for sharing.

Mattie'S Diner, 915 Hamilton St., Charlotte, NC 28206; (704) 376-1020; mattiesdiner.com; Diner; $. Located just across the street from the North Carolina Music Factory and open 24 hours a day, this retro diner was designed with those in search of comfort food in the wee hours in mind. However, whatever time of day you decide to slide into one of their red vinyl booths, you'll want to indulge in one of the thick juicy burgers served alongside their hot fries. Or, for the even bigger appetites, try dishes like the chicken-fried chicken topped in sawmill gravy or the pot roast served alongside roasted vegetables. Can't stay for long? Order one of the shakes to go. In fun flavors like PB & J and S'mores, these are so thick you'll want to ask for a spoon.

Mez, 210 E. Trade St., Charlotte, NC 28202; (704) 971-2400; mezcharlotte.com; American; $$$. On the top floor of the EpiCentre nightlife complex, this sleek restaurant offers a variety of options

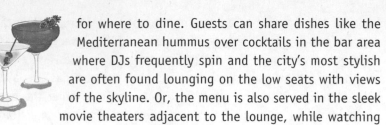

for where to dine. Guests can share dishes like the Mediterranean hummus over cocktails in the bar area where DJs frequently spin and the city's most stylish are often found lounging on the low seats with views of the skyline. Or, the menu is also served in the sleek movie theaters adjacent to the lounge, while watching Hollywood's latest flicks. And, of course, there's the traditional dining area where dishes like a pan-roasted salmon or short rib rigatoni can be lingered over and accompanied by candlelight.

Morton's Steakhouse, 227 W. Trade St., Ste. 150, Charlotte, NC 28202; (704) 333-2602; mortons.com/charlotte; Steakhouse; $$$. Like the others in this renowned steakhouse chain, Charlotte's version of Morton's is an upscale restaurant full of shiny mahogany and serving premium beef. Every cut of meat is presented in its raw form to the table prior to your meal (or seafood lovers can personally choose their live lobster) and each dish is prepared to perfection. Expect to have some of the best service in the city from dedicated servers—many of whom have been there for years. Lunchtime finds the dining room filled with important business lunches, while in the evening hours this spot is so popular for special occasions it's hard to sit through dinner without hearing at least one round of "Happy Birthday."

Pinky's Westside Grille, 1600 W. Morehead St., Charlotte, NC 28208; (704) 332-0402; eatatpinkys.com; Hamburgers; $. The first thing you'll likely notice about this casual burger joint is the colorful VW bug parked on its roof. Housed in a former auto shop, the bug pays homage to the spot's history. The second thing you should notice is the crispy, fried pickles. Served piping hot and piled high in a basket alongside a cool and creamy ranch, these salty chips draw crowds. While the menu offers salads and even falafel, it's the playfully named burgers and dogs that are favorites. If you're feeling adventurous, try the Ding Dong Style burger; served with crunchy peanut butter, Asian slaw, and *sriracha* sauce, it's spicy and unexpectedly delicious.

Press Wine and Food, 333 W. Trade St., Charlotte, NC 28202; (704) 370-3006; presswinefood.com; Sushi/Tapas; $$. This cozy wine bar is all about the vino and with more than 100 bottles of wine, all priced at retail price, you'll want to settle in for a nice long sip. There are overstuffed couches—and even board games—as well as casual cafe tables for enjoying small plates like sushi or paninis, but the best seat here is on the patio, where you can soak in skyline views while you enjoy your red or white. After spending some time perusing the walls lined with bottles to choose your pick for the evening, ask one of the knowledgeable servers for a perfect pairing. If you're lucky, they'll suggest one of the tasty sushi rolls. And while you might not expect a wine bar to be a prime lunch destination, Press's lunch counter serves up fresh, stuffed sandwiches fast, which means it's an easy choice for Uptown workers in search of a quick bite.

RiRa Irish Pub, 208 N. Tryon St., Charlotte, NC 28202; (704) 333-5554; rira.com; Irish/Pub; $$. While this pub may be part of a chain, it doesn't feel that way in Charlotte, where it has been a local favorite for years. After recent renovations the pub's upstairs features paintings of local notables under sparkling chandeliers, while the downstairs holds antiques shipped from Ireland. Many nights you'll find live music downstairs and if you're a fan of soccer, there's almost always a game of "football" on behind the bar. Stick to the Irish side of the menu with dishes like a hearty cottage pie or crispy fish and chips. And, of course, don't forget your pint of Guinness.

Room 112, 112 S. Tryon St., Ste. 101, Charlotte, NC 28284; (704) 335-7112; rm112.com; Sushi; $$. This small, corner restaurant is one of the city's best-kept secrets. Tucked just off the main intersection of Trade and Tryon Sts., Room 112 offers fresh, innovative sushi for some of the lowest prices in Uptown. Inside you'll find a small bar and intimate dining area, while just outside the door, tables sit fountain-side on the sidewalk. And while it tends to fill up during lunch time with those taking advantage of their sushi lunch combos, the sleek, red-accented dining area is quiet during the dinner hours, which means you can leisurely enjoy dishes like the perfectly seared Tuna Tataki or the rich Cherry Blossom roll featuring tempura shrimp and spicy tuna.

Rooster's Wood-Fired Kitchen, 150 N. College St., Charlotte, NC 28202; (704) 370-7667; roosterskitchen.com; Southern; $$$. Chef and Owner Jim Noble's new Uptown branch of his popular

SouthPark spot is a favorite for those in search of simply prepared dishes that allow the flavor of their produce to shine through. Dishes are served a la carte and you'll want to order several to share for the table. Even the simplest offerings, like Noble's Pan-Fried Corn offer a complex texture and taste. *Haricots verts* with garlic and herbs are the perfect mix of crisp and fragrant, while the butter beans are melt-in-your-mouth tender. The menu offers a variety of pastas, fish, and meat, but none are as fall-off-the-bone tender as the spit-fire-roasted chicken and pork shoulder options. Noble's signature barbecue sauce gives the half barbecue chicken a tangy sweet flavor that sets off his savory fresh veggies. When it's time to end the meal, there are several upscale—and delicious—offerings like a creamy panna cotta, but the milk shakes, named for Noble's daughter, are house-made and a sweet, playful completion to the meal. Additional location: 6601 Morrison Blvd., SouthPark, Charlotte, NC 28211; (704) 366-8688.

Ruth's Chris Steakhouse, 222 S. Tryon St., Charlotte, 28202; (704) 338-9444; ruthschris.com; Steakhouse; $$$. This place serves steak cooked in butter. It also has one of the city's best wine lists. Forget the diet and just go. You can luxuriate in the cherry-wood-paneled dining room with its granite floors and white tablecloths while you indulge. Staying away from red meat? Try the restaurant's barbecued shrimp. Sauteed New Orleans style in reduced white wine, butter, garlic, and spices, the tender, fresh shrimp are served atop a bed of fluffy mashed potatoes. See? You don't have to order the steak for a decadent dinner. Finish up your debauched dining streak with the Chocolate Sin Cake, dense chocolate and espresso cake topped in a thin sheen of rich chocolate and drizzled in strawberry sauce.

Savor on Morehead, 1404 W. Morehead St., Charlotte, NC 28208; (704) 334-0098; savoronmorehead.com; American; $$. This cozy Westside spot started as a quick lunch stop with fresh breads and creative sandwiches, but quickly expanded into a convivial dinner destination. The menu has a Southern slant with dishes like Sweet Tea Brined Grilled Pork Tenderloin, a tenderloin topped with peach chutney and served alongside grits and collards, or Savor's version of Shrimp and Grits featuring andouille sausage gravy and yellow stone-ground grits. But there's also an international twist with items like pad thai and a sweet-chili-glazed salmon with a distinctly Asian flavor. Whichever region you lean to for entrees, just don't skip dessert. The restaurant's elegant version of banana pudding is the perfect combination of creamy-meets-chunky and served with a delicate swirl of house-made whipped cream.

Urban Sip, 201 E. Trade St., Charlotte, NC 28202; (704) 547-2244; ritzcarlton.com; Tapas; $$. Sure, the 1st floor BLT Steak is tempting.

And yes, the lobby area Bar Cocoa chocolate shop is downright decadent. But the Ritz-Carlton's 15th floor Urban Sip may be the upscale hotel's best-kept secret. With stunning skyline views and a menu made to pair with more than 90 wines by the glass and 35 single-malt scotches, this is the kind of spot you'll want to settle in for an evening. The menu is predominantly small plates with offerings like olives seasoned in thyme from the hotel's rooftop garden or artisanal cheeses like the Carolina Moon from the nearby Chapel Hill Creamery. Want to enjoy the views before sundown? Urban Sip also frequently offers afternoon tea complete with decadent finger sandwiches like miniature lobster rolls and smoked salmon.

Vapiano, 201 S. Tryon St., Charlotte, NC 28202; (704) 332-2440; vapianointernational.com; Italian; $$. This Tryon Street restaurant is hard to categorize. It's an international chain, but it serves gourmet Italian dishes—and requires that you wait in line to order them. If you haven't been to one of its other locations, the system here can be a little confusing. Diners are given a card upon entering, which is then swiped at each food station to record orders. When you leave, your total order rings up at the door. Unusual though it may be, this tasty Italian fare makes it worth it. The lines are usually the longest at the pasta and pizza stations, and with good reason. Large, made-to-order pizzas come in savory combinations like a barbecue-chicken pizza with Gouda and fresh cilantro. And while Vapiano's chic dining room lends itself to nighttime dining, it's also a perfect spot for a quick midday lunch. For those looking for a lighter meal, offerings like a spicy orange fennel salad with glazed shrimp are perfect. Just don't leave without ordering your "Dolci." Desserts are served in small glasses and are each $3.75. The panna cotta, featuring cooked cream, vanilla beans, and a fresh, seasonal fruit topping is as close to Italy as you're likely to come for under $4.

VBGB Beer Hall and Garden, 920 Hamilton St., Charlotte, NC 28206; (704) 333-4111; vbgbuptown.com; German; $. You're unlikely to find a better spot in town to spend a warm evening than the huge patio at this popular beer garden. Strung with white lights and within earshot of concerts happening at Music Factory's amphitheater, the vibe here is as laid back as they come. Beers are a mix of local and international and can be ordered by the pitcher at either the interior bar or a small window facing the beer garden. The selection changes frequently, but is always extensive enough to satisfy even the choosiest beer snob. The food, as you might expect, is designed to pair well with the brews. Order it at a small counter and you'll likely be impressed with how tasty dishes as simple as a jumbo soft pretzel or hot dog can be. Some of the offerings are actually surprisingly complex (think quinoa salad in a lime vinaigrette or potato latkes with sour cream dip), but they're all best when paired with a cold pint on a warm night.

Vida Cantina, 210 E. Trade St., Charlotte, NC 28202; (704) 971-8433; vidacantina.com; Mexican; $$$. If you enjoy people watching, you won't find a better patio in town than this corner of

Trade and College. Located on a corner of Uptown's busy EpiCentre complex, Vida stays busy with stylish locals seeking its well-crafted tequila cocktails, tacos, burritos, and larger plates. While they have typical offerings of queso and guacamole, skip them in favor of the more creative lump crab nachos or ceviche cocktail. And don't worry about feeling guilty adding these on to your cocktail—Vida's signature skinny margarita offers all of the flavor and power of a regular margarita with none of the cloying sweetness for only 100 calories. This is especially good because it means more room for indulging in Vida's luxe entrees like the grilled lime marinated shrimp topped with garlic and lime, or the slow-cooked pork simmer with poblano chiles and served with a warm, flour tortilla. While you're indulging, don't forget dessert. Specifically, don't forget to order the authentic Mexican churro; deep fried and served with a hot-chocolate dipping sauce it's the perfect end or—if you're off to EpiCentre—beginning to the evening.

Villa Francesca, 321 N. Caldwell St., Charlotte, NC 28202; (704) 333-7447; villafrancescacharlotte.com; Italian; $$. If you're going to be eating authentic New York pizza, it should be from a casual place where the owner's name is Louis and you're unlikely to find him without his Yankees cap. The pizzas—which you can smell from a block away—are the kind where the oversize slices need folding to fit in your mouth and you'll want extra napkins for wiping up when you're finished. If you're only ordering one, order the

Grandma Pizza. It comes in a 16-by-16-inch square with extra thin crust, plenty of fresh mozzarella, and the special "Grandma" sauce, which tastes part marinara, part Italian heaven.

Landmarks

Alexander Michael's Restaurant and Tavern, 401 W. 9th St., Charlotte, NC 28202; (704) 332-6789; almikestavern.com; Pub; $$. Affectionately known as Al Mike's, this cozy tavern opened almost 30 years ago in the historic Fourth Ward neighborhood. The bar is actually made from solid oak doors that were in the Independence Building in Uptown before it was torn down in the early '80s. And most nights many in the crowd are locals from the neighborhood who come to catch a game or grab a pint. The menu offers a wide range, from quesadillas and nachos to catfish and steak. But the standout is the traditional stroganoff, a rich mix of mushrooms and beef in a red wine and sour cream sauce over rotini pasta—the perfect comfort food for a chilly evening.

McNinch House, 511 N. Church St., Charlotte, NC 28202; (704) 332-6159; mcninchhouserestaurant.com; French; $$$. Rumor has it that many of the city's biggest deals have gone down in the hushed rooms of this elegant historic mansion, where the French-influenced menu is fixed price each night. Reservations are a must and before you arrive, you'll be called with questions about food allergies, seating preferences, and preferred dishes. Upon arrival guests are greeted warmly as if entering a private home before being escorted to candlelit tables with the owner's own family china. Dishes are exquisite with the foie gras and duck being top choices many nights. Still not feeling completely spoiled? Ladies are given a single-stem red rose as their parting gift each night.

Mert's Heart and Soul Restaurant, 214 N. College St., Charlotte, NC 28202; (704) 342-4222; mertscharlotte.com; Southern; $. While this casual restaurant has only been around since 1998, it has quickly found a permanent spot in the hearts of locals. Maybe it's because the owners frequently donate their food to local charitable organizations. Or maybe it's because it's beloved by famed Bank of America CEO Hugh McColl. But it seems most likely that it's because of its scrumptious soul food options like creamy mac and cheese, fried green tomatoes, blackened pork chops, and stewed okra and tomatoes. If you only order one thing, make it the salmon cakes. Made with poached fresh salmon blended with celery, onions, and peppers and served alongside a creamy remoulade, this dish will tempt you to repeat your order as soon as you've finished your first.

The World Famous Open Kitchen, 1318 W. Morehead St., Charlotte, NC 28208; (704) 375-7449; Italian; $$. Ok, so the name may be a little presumptuous, but if it's not world famous, it probably should be. Known as the first place in North Carolina to ever serve pizza, the restaurant's ambience feels like stepping back in time 40 years. Talk to any longtime Charlottean about where they ate growing up, and it's likely that this spot will get a mention. Walls covered in black and white photos evoke nostalgia while hearty servings of pizza and pasta prompt mouth watering. The pizza is decent and the meatballs are savory, but really, if you're here, what you're looking for a taste of is historic Charlotte.

Specialty Stores, Markets & Producers

Bar Cocoa, 201 E. Trade St., Charlotte, NC 29202; (704) 547-2244; ritzcarlton.com. Just off the lobby lounge of the swanky Ritz-Carlton, this small bar offers the chance to sit and indulge in chocolate treats or grab an irresistible confection to take with you. A colorful display case tempts with an array of chocolates, from decadent truffles to slices of rich pastries. The Tahitian caramel chocolate is a must with creamy milk chocolate over a buttery caramel and vanilla. And even if you're on the run, pause for a cup of the Bar Cocoa hot chocolate—a rich drink that tastes as if someone melted a candy bar in a mug. Want to create your own confections? Check the website for upcoming classes taught by the hotel's talented pastry chef.

Center City Green Market, 200 S. Tryon St., (704) 332-2227; centercitygreenmarket.com. Located on the plaza at Trade and

7TH STREET PUBLIC MARKET

When Mayor Anthony Foxx cut the ribbon on this city market in December 2011, he called it an incubator for local food businesses. It's a new concept for a city like Charlotte where steakhouse chains used to rule the dining scene. Here you'll find small local vendors often selling from small local farms.

A walk through the market is enough to get anyone excited about the region's local food scene. Set in a former grocery store adjacent to the city's light rail, the space is bright and open. A small bakery offers muffins and pastries next to a start-up coffee shop serving fresh-brewed cups of joe. Across the aisle you'll find a veggie stand offering seasonal vegetables from a variety of local farms. And a few tables down, you'll find a woman selling freshly made, local cheeses across from another selling herbs and seasonings.

It may look a little like a farmers' market at first glance, but don't mistake it for one. It's different because many of the food and drinks here are simply made locally rather than grown locally. Plus, 7th Street Public Market is open year-round, which means this local fare is available any time you want it. 225 E. 6th St., Charlotte, NC 28203; (704) 230-4346; 7thstreetmarket.com.

Tryon Sts., this urban market caters a variety of goods ranging from produce and meats to baked goods and sweets. Open from the beginning of May through Labor Day weekend, the market features fare from local farms and residents. It's not the city's biggest or best farmers' market, but the combination of its urban setting among skyscrapers and in the shadow of international banks, as well as its wide variety of products makes it a charming stop to pick up a bite. Plus, check the Twitter handles of your favorite food trucks before you make the trip. Many days they're pulled up here offering their freshly made fare alongside the vendors.

Dean & Deluca, 201 S. Tryon St., Charlotte, NC 28202; (704) 377-0037; deandeluca.com. While the Uptown version of this upscale grocery chain isn't as large as its SouthPark sister—or even the Stonecrest version in South Charlotte, it does offer some of the same fine food and wine selections. Your best bet here is in the prepared food section where you'll find the shop's signature sushi, sandwiches, and salads, all perfect for picnicking in one of the nearby urban parks. If you're stopping in at lunch on a weekday, just be prepared for lines. This is a popular stop for those seeking a quick, fresh bite before heading back to work.

Dilworth & South End

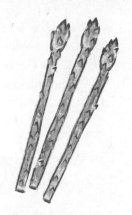

Two of Charlotte's most historic neighborhoods, these charming areas border each other just south of Uptown. And while their rich histories are similar in some ways (Dilworth grew because of its streetcar line and South End because of its railroad line), they're also notably different.

Dilworth is characterized by quiet bungalow-filled neighborhoods with sidewalk-lined streets shaded by oak trees. Neighbors chat from front porches, and restaurants and shops in the area have the feeling of being a spot where the locals know the owner—and one another. Dilworth has been popular for years, but South End's history tells a different story. Its railroad originally drew a booming textile industry around its tracks. But after the industry suffered in the 1970s and 1980s, so did the neighborhood. These days, though, Charlotte's subway system, the Light Rail, runs on the tracks and the historic mills are again filled—this time with bustling restaurants, bars, shops, and condos.

Now, the bordering neighborhoods are home to some of the city's most popular destinations for dining. From a cozy British pub just off the tracks to an elegant bistro housed in a historic church, you'll find plenty of character—and good food—in this section of town.

Foodie Faves

Bad Daddy's Burger Bar, 1626 East Blvd., Dilworth, Charlotte, NC 28203; (704) 714-4888; baddaddysburgerbar.com; Hamburgers; $. Ask any Charlottean to name their favorite restaurants and it's likely that Bad Daddy's will make the list. This casual and convivial burger destination has a line out the door many nights as fans wait to enjoy one of its famed burgers, salads, or shakes. And in good weather, you can almost certainly expect to wait for a patio seat. But one taste of one of these juicy burgers, a side of sweet potato fries, or the beloved tater tots and you'll get it. The best way to arrive at Bad Daddy's is hungry and thirsty. Start with one of their more than 20 beers on tap (if you happen to already know which burger you're ordering, they'll tell you the best for pairing). Then dig into the fried pickles appetizer featuring hot, salty strands of fried pickles served alongside a creamy and cool ranch for dipping. When it comes to both burgers and salads, you can create your own from a variety of meat, bread, and topping options. But, many of the most creative—and best—burger options have already been created as Bad Daddy's specialties. Take, for example, the Ahi Tuna Burger featuring a tuna burger marinating in ginger, lime and soy, then topped with creamy wasabi mayo and a crispy peanut soy Asian slaw. Or, for a Parisian-inspired burger, try the Frenchie, a turkey burger topped with melted brie cheese, sweet applewood smoked bacon, tender grilled apples and a savory garlic mayo. Pair these burgers with one of the sides like sweet potato fries, onion straws, house-made potato chips, or tater tots. Still hungry? Wash it all down with one of the soft-serve ice cream milk shakes in creative flavors like PB & J or Snickers.

Big Ben British Pub, 2000 South Blvd., South End, Charlotte, NC 28203; (704) 817-9697; bigbenpub.com; Pub; $$. Brush up on the lyrics to "God Save the Queen," your knowledge of soccer, and your appreciation of traditional British fare at this cozy Atherton Mill pub just off the light rail. If you go on a dreary day and order the cottage pie alongside a pint of Boddingtons or Newcastle Brown, you can almost imagine you're in a London corner pub. One of the only spots in town serving a traditional English breakfast, in this casual restaurant you'll find the British favorite: two eggs, an English banger, baked beans, potatoes, grilled tomato, grilled mushrooms, and toast. Enjoy it with a pot of English tea and you're as close to Britain is it gets this side of the pond. The lunch and dinner menus stick to traditional as well with English favorites like bangers 'n' mash, shepherds pie, Southend Haddock and Chips, and even roast lamb and beef, perfect for a cool Sunday afternoon. For the full experience, end the meal with a dessert like sticky toffee pudding or spotted dick. And, like at any good pub, the evenings here are often lively with patrons taking advantage of drink specials like $4 pints—and televisions for cheering on your favorite team (soccer, of course).

Bonterra Dining and Wine Room, 1829 Cleveland Ave., Dilworth, Charlotte, NC 28203; (704) 333-9463; bonterradining.com; American/French/Steakhouse; $$$. When the signature menu item is fried lobster tail and the menu has hundreds of wines by the glass, you know you're in a restaurant that's a step above the rest. At Bonterra the trend continues with its elegant setting—the restaurant is housed in a historic Dilworth church—and its impressive cheese and charcuterie selection. Plus, there are more than 200 wines offered by the glass as well as an additional 300 available in bottles from the cellar. The menu's entire first section is actually dedicated to "Food for Wine." Enjoy locally cured charcuteries, olives, and an impressive selection of cheese ranging from international (*pecorino toscano* from Italy) to a semi-firm cow's milk from Georgia. If you're looking for an elegant spot for drinks and bites, the bar is perfect for enjoying a glass of wine alongside these pairings. If it's dinner you're seeking, though, settle in with starters like pork belly bro-chette or the duck confit spring roll before moving on to specialties like the slow-braised lamb shank or osso bucco short rib. And, of course, if you're a fan of lobster, you can't miss the fried lobster tail. Lightly fried tender meat is served alongside a sweet and sour mustard aioli and a wildflower and honey soy reduction. Prefer not to pay $45 for an entree? The dish comes in a smaller version under Starters for just a $21 taste.

Brixx Wood-Fired Pizza, 1801 Scott Ave., Dilworth, Charlotte, NC 28203; (704) 376-1000; brixxpizza.com; Italian; $$. If you happen to pass this popular pizza joint on a warm evening, the first thing you'll notice is the packed patio just off East Boulevard. The next thing you'll notice is the unmistakable fragrance of fresh, brick-oven pizza. Dilworth was the first location for this chain that has grown across the Southeast and it's easy to see what made it successful when you're indulging in these thick slices. In addition to all your usual favorites (think Margherita, Hawaiian, and *quatro formaggio)* the Brixx also offers plenty of unique signature pizzas worth trying. Dig into options such as the Pear and Gorgonzola topped with cara-melized onions and toasted walnuts or the Pimento Cheese Pizza made with jalapeño pimento cheese, roasted red peppers, crumbled bacon, and spinach leaves. Plus, the restaurant makes it easy for everyone to enjoy a slice with vegan and even gluten-free options. And while pizza is the star here, there are plenty of other choices like sandwiches made using freshly baked focaccia bread or salads featuring locally grown vegetables. Whatever you choose, enjoy it alongside one of their local craft brews or a playful cocktail like the Pizza-tini—chilled Grey Goose and dry vermouth with two olives stuffed with spicy pepperoni.

Brookberry Farm, 1257 East Blvd., Dilworth, Charlotte, NC 28203; (704) 334-6528; berrybrookfarm.com; Vegetarian; $. With its red roof and log cabin-esque fascade in the middle of the bustling Dilworth neighborhood, this natural-food haven will likely catch your eye. Founded in 1972 the pantry offers groceries and produce alongside natural health and beauty aids. But its best-kept secret is its juice bar where in addition to fresh smoothies, you'll find a variety of sandwiches and soups offered daily. Choices like bean burritos, herb tofu sandwiches, tofu hot dogs, and veggie pimento sandwiches are among the favorites here. On cool days stop in for one of the hot and healthy soups like a white bean black olive, Thai curry sweet potato, or wild mushroom. The smoothies are the real stars. You can have them made with soy milk and they come loaded with fresh fruits and veggies as well as hard-to-find organic flavors like ginger. While there is no seating inside, the front porch offers a cozy porch swing and you're within walking distance of several of the neighborhood's nicest parks, perfect for enjoying your healthy meal in the sun.

Cantina 1511, 1511 East Blvd., Dilworth, Charlotte, NC 28203; (704) 331-9222; cantina1511restaurant.com; Mexican; $$. Before Mexican restaurants began cropping up on seemingly every corner in Charlotte, this was the place to go when you were craving tableside guacamole, premium margaritas, and a taste of mole. Today, it's still an exceedingly popular spot where the bar is crowded most weekends with those in search of one of their signature cocktails alongside crispy, house-made tortilla chips and tomato salsa. The dining room is always bustling during both the lunch and dinner hours with guests enjoying dishes ranging from traditional tacos and quesadillas, to the harder-to-find-this-side-of-the-Rio-Grande options like Salmon al Pastor, an *achiote-* and lime-seared salmon served with roasted pineapple, black-bean tostada, pico de gallo, and grilled scallions. For a decadent twist on your typical Mexican order, try the Cantina 1511 Fundido made with imported Mexican cheeses melted with fresh herbs, jalapeño bacon, roasted pineapple and onions, and served with house-made flour tortillas. The best suggestion for dining here is to get there early—especially if you're hoping for a seat on the street-side porch. You can't make reservations for outside seating and diners tend to linger there. Of course, once you're there with your tangy margarita in hand, you'll understand why.

Cluck 'n Cup, 2135 Southend Dr., South End, Charlotte, NC 28203; (980) 207-2536; cluckncup.com; American; $. Sure, coffee and chicken may seem like an odd menu combination, but consider the cozy factor with each and you'll start to understand this charming South End spot. Tucked in a shopping center off South Boulevard, the cafe and coffee shop would be easy to miss, but one taste of their famed chicken potpies and you won't soon forget it. The menu is varied and homemade, offering options like a tasty spinach and black bean quesadilla, but if you like chicken potpies at all, you've got to try this one. Topped with a flaky golden crust, the pie is stuffed full of chunks of white meat, corn, carrots, peas, and beans all in a creamy sauce. While the pies are made fresh daily, the best time to enjoy one is on a Wednesday when they're offered with a side (definitely try the house-made broccoli cas-serole) and drink for $5.99. You can order it in and enjoy it in the poultry-themed interior complete with ceramic roosters and glass chickens. Or, if you prefer to enjoy the dish's down-home comfort at home, Cluck 'n Cup offers take-and-bake family-size pies perfect for heating up on chilly nights.

Copper, 311 East Blvd., Dilworth, Charlotte, NC 28203; (704) 333-0063; copperrestaurant.com; Indian; $$$. While the exterior of this sophisticated Dilworth spot doesn't look like your typical Indian restaurant, the fragrant scents of curry and spices emanating from its kitchen give it away. Located in a historic East Boulevard bun-galow, the old boarding house's interior features brightly colored rooms with Sanskrit inscriptions on the walls. During the day, the bright front room with its tall windows offers views of the busy street, while in the evening, the candlelit rooms toward the back of the home lend themselves to intimate dinners. An international wine list, including wines from India, pairs well with traditional offerings like a creamy *tikka masala* featuring chunks of chicken

'Cue Culture

There's no doubt that people in North Carolina are serious about their barbecue. The division over the tomato base used in Lexington-style barbecue and the vinegar base of Eastern-style barbecue is the kind of thing that causes legitimate arguments. And don't even get North Carolinians started on those crazy South Carolinians with their mustard-based 'cue.

Nothing fires up local culinary pride like the discussion of true slow smoking over a wood pit versus using an electric pit. Old timers and traditionalists even go so far as insisting on examining those wood piles you see outside of many of the state's barbecue joints. Find a spider web? This thing is just for show.

Charlotte itself isn't known for its barbecue—partially because health code inside the city limits prohibits some of the cooking that those 'cue connoisseurs swear by. However, from new restaurants set to open soon in Uptown to popular barbecue-focused festivals, the city is jumping on to the state's favorite meat.

And no neighborhood has led the charge as much as South End where you'll find **Bill Spoon's BBQ** (5524 South Blvd., South End, Charlotte, NC 28217; 704-525-8865; spoonsbarbecue.com), long known as the city's top spot for whole hogs, as well as **Mac's Speed Shop** (2511 South Blvd., South End, Charlotte, NC 28203; 704-522-6227; macspeedshop.com), a place where barbecue paired with beer and bikes means crowds lining up for swine. The more recent addition of **Sauceman's** (228 West Blvd., South End, Charlotte, NC 28203; 704-333-7070; saucemans.com) puts a contemporary spin on an old favorite, but there's no denying the tender texture and smoky flavor of its authentic pulled pork.

Wherever you choose to indulge in this local flavor, just be sure to pair it with a scoop of coleslaw, hot hush puppies, and a large glass of sweet and Southern iced tea.

in a semisweet sauce perfect for sopping up with the garlic naan. However, this menu goes beyond your typical curry house fare with sophisticated, contemporary offers like lamb chops in a mustard ginger marinade topped with a sweet pomegranate curry. It's an upscale menu and atmosphere, and the prices reflect that, but stop by for the weekday lunch and you'll find the same savory fare at lunch-size prices.

Dilworth Neighborhood Grille, 911 East Morehead St., Dilworth, Charlotte, NC 28204; (704) 377-3808; neighborhoodgrille.com; American; $$. This two-story grill and bar is known for being a great place to catch a game. Whether you're pulling up a stool to the bar to watch the Panthers play just up the street in Bank of America Stadium or squeezing into a booth to catch the Tarheels shoot baskets, many nights you'll find a lively crowd pulling for the home team. Friendly servers and cold beverages are their specialty, but you'll find plenty of tasty fare as well. The grill gets packed during lunch hour with fans of its burgers and sandwiches like the Bendert Burger Wrap, a seasoned burger wrapped in a flour tortilla stuffed with cheddar jack cheese, lettuce, tomato, and ranch dressing. And while the dinner menu is varied, ranging from pizzas to shrimp and grits, there are several entrees worth the visit, including a few savory pastas like the primavera chicken pasta with tomatoes, spinach, and Portobello mush-rooms in a white-wine butter sauce. If you happen to be looking for a good spot for breakfast, DNG offers a tasty morning menu with choices like crab cakes and eggs or chocolate-chip pancakes. And, of course, its location makes it a great spot to stop in before the game up the street, so expect to see plenty of blue and black digging into omelets on game day.

Dolce Ristorante, 1710 Kenilworth Ave., Dilworth, Charlotte, NC 28203; (704) 332-7525; dolceristorante.net; Italian; $$$. Its corner-of-a-strip-mall location is deceptive when it comes to this fabulous Italian restaurant. Step inside this family-run trattoria and you'll find an elegant ambience and some of the city's best pasta dishes served alongside an all-Italian wine list. Warm and friendly servers offer glasses of sparking Prosecco to start your meal and it pairs well with appetizers like the Positano mussels sautéed with garlic and in a sauce so delicious you'll insist on using the crusty, freshly baked bread for sopping it up. But let's get to the important part: the pasta. A Bolognese ragu features slow-braised veal and pork tossed in thick, tender spaghetti noodles, while a cannelloni offering is studded with fresh milky ricotta, spinach, and mascarpone cheese and then drenched in a Parmesan cream sauce. If you only go once, though, go on a Tuesday when the chef makes fresh gnocchi. The airy pillows of potato pasta pair perfectly with the butter-sage sauce for a meal that is both decadent and light. And, just as when you're in Italy, lingering over dessert should be mandatory. The tiramisu is as creamy as you'd imagine, but it's the house-made gelato that is a must. Dolce actually began as a simple gelato shop and the dessert offering in flavors like rum raisin or almond reminds you of its sweet roots.

East Boulevard Bar and Grill, 1315 East Blvd., Dilworth, Charlotte, NC 28203; (704) 332-2414; ebbandg.com; American; $. Formerly located in an older home just a few blocks away, this bar and grill has upgraded to its new location in the center of Dilworth. The best time to visit is on warm days when the garage door windows are rolled up and the entire dining room feels like an alfresco experience. For the most part, the menu is your basic bar food, but there are a few exceptions like the sushi-grade ahi tuna tartare tower featuring fresh avocado and wasabi aioli or the roasted garlic herb pork loin served with a Dijon honey au jus. The best items are the more casual offerings like their chopped rib eye Philly cheesesteak topped with melted provolone cheese and grilled onions and served on a freshly baked hoagie. To really indulge, enjoy them with a side of the signature home fries or hand-cooked potato chips. The offerings from the bar are mostly the expected, but ask your server for drink specials because they tend to run ones you won't want to miss.

Ed's Tavern, 2200 Park Rd., Dilworth, Charlotte, NC 28203; (704) 335-0033; edstavern.com; Pub; $. Located in a mostly residential area of Dilworth, this bar is a favorite for locals in the neighborhood. Originally built in 1921 the building has been many things, including a hardware store (the neon Martin's Hardware Store sign still hangs in the window). Exposed brick walls, well-worn wood floors, and antique lights give this a casual vibe. On most nights you'll find it full of patrons shooting pool, playing games, listening to live music, and engaging in one of the city's most popular music trivia nights. With more than 25 beers on tap daily, this is a favorite for locals from the neighborhood in search of a cold one. The menu reflects a spot dedicated to its casual atmosphere and strong drinks with popular options like nachos, cheese fries, onion rings, burgers, and wings. There are, however, a few unexpected finds like the fried golden brown green beans with a cool ranch dressing or the pecan pear salad topped with blue cheese and candied pecans. Whatever you order, enjoy it alongside a pint and soak up the friendly atmosphere of this laid-back bar.

Fiamma Restaurant, 2418 Park Rd., Dilworth, Charlotte, NC 28203; (704) 333-3062; fiamma-restaurant.com; Italian; $$$. Ah, Tuscany. Finding a taste of one of Italy's most beautiful regions in the middle of North Carolina wasn't easy—until Fiamma. This elegant Italian restaurant offers Tuscan wines alongside dishes like thin-crust pizzas made using imported cow's milk cheese and white truffle oil or rigatoni pasta with sautéed eggplant in a tomato sauce with fresh ricotta. But the kitchen's talent really shines through best on the "Il Pesce" part of the menu. A delicate red snapper is sautéed with white wine, light tomato broth, olives, and capers, leaving the fresh seafood flavor fully intact, while a roasted Norwegian salmon is finished with a tangy, buttery *salmoriglio* sauce that's incredibly light and fresh. The menu isn't long, but each option is exquisitely prepared so finding an order shouldn't be difficult. And knowing what to finish with is easy. The espresso evokes images of lingering in a Tuscan cafe and with its dark, rich flavor; you'll be happy to do just that.

The Flying Biscuit Cafe, 4241 Park Rd., Dilworth, Charlotte, NC 28209; (704) 714-3400; flyingbiscuit.com; American/Breakfast/ Southern; $$. The decor is crazy and the lines are usually long— especially for the weekend brunch crowd. But don't let anything deter you from digging in to these fun and delicious breakfast offerings. This Atlanta-based restaurant (there are two in Charlotte) serves breakfast, lunch, and dinner, but it's the breakfast-all-day menu that seems to be a favorite. Check out amusingly named dishes like the Egg-ceptional Eggs, featuring two large farm-fresh eggs over-medium served on black-bean cakes and topped with oven-roasted tomatillo salsa, feta cheese, and sour cream. It's a Southern-meets-Mexican treat that shows up a typical omelet every time. If you're in the mood for something sweet, try the organic oatmeal pancakes. Topped with warm peach compote and served with maple syrup, they're good enough that you'll be tempted to lick your plate even after finishing all three. And if you must stray from breakfast, be sure to try the fried green tomatoes made with seasoned cornmeal and topped with cashew-jalapeño relish and goat cheese. But, whatever you do, make sure your meal includes one of the thick and fluffy oversized biscuits. Enjoy them hot with the homemade cranberry apple butter and you'll understand those crowds. Additional location: 7930 Rea Rd., Stonecrest, Charlotte, NC 28277; (704) 295-4440.

Fran's Filling Station, 2410 Park Rd., Dilworth, Charlotte, NC 28203; (704) 372-2009; fransfillingstation.com; American/ Southern; $$. This is the neighborhood restaurant every neighborhood wishes it had. While this Dilworth spot is relatively new, an evening or lunch hour spent here makes it feel as if it's been around for years. Friendly servers chat with regulars and patrons ask about their favorite specials. This place is about as comfortable and cozy as it gets with servers wearing amusing T-shirts with quotes like "Note to Fran: Relax" and colorful chairs huddled around cafe tables. For the most part this spot caters to families, couples, and friends looking for good food. And good food isn't hard to find here. Take the famed bacon-wrapped tater tots—dipped in a sweet glaze. Or try the pan-fried sweet corn nuggets; hot, crunchy, and perfect for pairing with the cool goat cheese ranch dressing. While sandwiches like a hot turkey featuring melted brie, apples, and apricot sauce, or a lemon chicken salad in a light lemon aioli, dominate the lunch menu (Fran is known for her fresh, tasty breads), dinner is full of those dishes you're always craving. Look for a rich meatloaf accompanied by creamy mashed potatoes or tender mussels swimming in a coconut and red curry sauce. And if you're seeking a really fun twist, go on Friday nights when Fran's goes south of the border with offerings like pork carnitas and margaritas that could rival any Mexican spot around. See Executive Chef and Owner Fran Scibelli's recipe for **Metropolitan Meatloaf** on p. 254.

Fuel Pizza Cafe, 1801 South Blvd., Dilworth, Charlotte, NC 28203; (704) 335-7375; fuelpizza.com; Italian; $$. This pizza chain is a longtime local favorite and the shop at the corner of South Blvd. and East Blvd. is no exception. If you're in the mood for delivery, but want something a step up from Papa John's or Dominoes, Fuel offers tasty pizzas with toppings like sun-dried tomato and pesto. (They also have gluten-free versions of their pizzas, which are often hard to find). You can pop in for take out or enjoy the pizza in the shop, where you can order pizzas by the so-large-you-have-to-fold-them-to-eat-them slices. At the restaurant you'll often find Motown playing and you can finish your meal with one of the $3 Brad's Cupcakes or the doughy cinnamon knots. Filled with families on the weekends, this is an easy place to grab a pie and enjoy the casual vibe.

Greek Isles, 200 E. Bland St., South End, Charlotte, NC 28203; (704) 444-9000; greekislesrestaurant.com; Greek; $$. When this South End spot opened in 2004, it solved the city's need for a restaurant dedicated to authentic Greek fare. Owned by the Photopoulos family, the restaurant offers fresh seafood prepared in Greek fashion, classics like spanakopita, plenty of lamb dishes, and, of course, a sticky, melt-in-your-mouth baklava. Start with an appetizer featuring a variety of spreads including potato whipped with garlic and an eggplant puree, perfect for smearing on the fresh pitas. Then move on to the Santorini pasta made with fresh linguine tossed in a zesty tomato sauce with tender shrimp alongside. Among the fish dishes the Bacalao, a salted, lightly breaded, pan-fried cod topped with marinated beets and potato-garlic spread stands out. And, of course, there are plenty of your favorite Greek specialties like a gyro pita featuring seasoned ground lamb and beef tucked into a warm pita with feta, tomato, onion, and a creamy tzatziki sauce. Or, try the dolmades, hand-rolled grape leaves stuffed with ground beef, rice, and herbs. And whether you're there for lunch or dinner, don't leave without some of that baklava. Delicate layers of fillo dough are coated in walnuts, cinnamon, and honey, and for the really decadent version, order it *"me pagoto"* with vanilla ice cream drizzled in chocolate and caramel.

Icehouse, 2100 South Blvd., South End, Charlotte, NC 28203; (704) 375-1128; icehousesouthend.com; American/Hamburger; $. Just off the light rail, this large venue in South End's Atherton Mills has become a favorite for those looking for a quick lunch or a great place to watch the game later in the evening. The interior features dark woods and frosted blues, as well as a long stretch of cooler brimming with ice—and beers—behind the bar. Plus, 20 televisions make it impossible to find a bad spot to catch what's on. A large deck also lends itself to alfresco drinks and bites during good weather. The menu features all the tasty fare you'd hope for in a bar, but with the occasional international twist like the sesame- and ancho-seared tuna tacos topped with Asian slaw and wasabi cream, or the Thai noodle salad packed with shaved cabbage, carrots, cucumbers, and fried wonton strips in a ginger-peanut vinaigrette. But, for the best options for pairing with one of the literally ice-cold brews, look under the sliders and burgers. The slider sampler platter may be your best deal if you've got a buddy for sharing. Featuring three beef, three pork, and three buffalo chicken sliders, as well as fries or house-made potato chips, you won't find a better dish for downing while you watch the game and sip your brew.

Kabob Grill, 1235 East Blvd., Dilworth, Charlotte, NC 28203; (704) 371-8984; kabobgrill.com; Mediterranean; $. Start with the hummus. For that matter, go for the hummus. It's smooth, creamy, and full of rich flavor. Paired with fresh veggies and thick, warm pitas, this house-made dish alone is worth the trip to this small Mediterranean restaurant tucked away in a Dilworth strip mall. Options like a beef gyro and a falafel wrap are also top sellers for good reason and while it's a cozy, friendly spot to sit and even offers a few outside tables, this is also a great place to grab a wrap—or some honey-soaked, pistachio nut–dotted baklava—to go. However, if you're settling in for the full meal, try the lentil and vegetable soup followed by the lamb kabob. The kabob is served with a savory side of tabbouleh and is a specialty you won't find many places in town.

Lebowski's Neighborhood Grill, 1524 East Blvd., Dilworth, Charlotte, NC 28203; (704) 370-1177; lebowskisgrillandpub.com; American/Hamburgers; $. On a stretch of East Blvd. with a fair share of bars and pubs, this grill stands apart from the rest. It's a cozy spot, owned and run by a father and his daughters, where the music is usually indie and the crowd is generally families or friends catching a game and drinking a beer. Charlotte has quite a few upstate New York transplants and they often flock to this spot for its Beef on Weck, a Buffalo, New York, favorite made with thin-sliced roast beef piled high on a freshly made weck roll. The menu also includes popular chicken wings in five different sauces including a tangy jerkiyaki and a traditional kickin' q. The burgers include creative topping offerings like the Tuscan-style burger with tomato bruschetta, pesto aioli, and melted provolone, or the seriously tasty jerk-style burger featuring pineapple salsa, jerkiyaki glaze, and melted Pepper Jack cheese. Whether you're seeking a quick lunch or looking for a place to linger over a few drinks with dinner, this inviting grill is worth stopping by.

The Liberty, 1812 South Blvd., South End, Charlotte, NC 28203; (704) 332-8830; thelibertycharlotte.com; Pub; $$. This South End restaurant, owned and run by two veterans on the Charlotte culinary scene, is serious about both its beer and its food. A large bar area features walls covered in vintage beer advertisements, elegant wood paneling, and a fireplace that gives it the feeling of a traditional English pub. And, with more than 20 beers on tap plus 50 by the bottle, including hard-to-find imports and top locally brewed offerings, this place is a haven for beer lovers. But foodies get their fill here as well. The dining room features walls created to look like the bubbles in beer and warm-colored accents, giving it a cozy ambience. Pleasantly busy at both lunch and dinner, the menu here changes frequently, but offers many highlights that show up often. If they're on the menu when you're there, these are a few musts: the pork belly sliders made with the tender meat and topped with a sweet vanilla bean apple butter; the chicken and dumplings prepared in a semisweet sauce; and, possibly most noteworthy, The Lucky Gastro Pig, a large serving of slow-roasted pork shoulder accompanied by delicate crepes, pickled pineapple, spicy peanuts, jalapeños, and lettuce. It seems like a strange way to eat pork—especially in the middle of barbecue country—but once you've tried your pork wrapped in a crepe with pickled pineapple, you may never go back to the traditional.

Luna's Living Kitchen, 2102 South Blvd., South End, Charlotte, NC 28203; (704) 333-0008; lunaslivingkitchen.com; Vegan; $$. Queen City vegans rejoiced when this South End restaurant opened up shop in Atherton Mill. Not only is the food vegan, it's also raw. This means that not only does the Lunasagna not have meat or cheese, it's actually made entirely from uncooked veggies. In place of noodles there's thinly sliced zucchini and sun-dried tomato sauce subs in for a meat sauce while a vegan mixture of ground cashews and basil creates a cheese-like substance. But while it may not be for those who prefer their food hot and meaty, Luna's has a devoted following who flock to their counter-service restaurant

for dishes like the Tres Marias Veggie
Burger, a quinoa-kamut burger served on
local vegan bread, or the West Coast Wrap
featuring sweet curry, sprouts, avocados,
bell peppers, tomatoes, and cucumbers
wrapped in collard leaves. One of the small

restaurant's best dishes may be its tricolor hummus. Three creamy
hummus options made with lemon-parsley, chipotle peppers, and
curry are served alongside an organic cranberry-walnut baguette in
a dish that tastes way too good to be this healthy.

Mac's Speed Shop, 2511 South Blvd., South End, Charlotte, NC;
28203; (704) 522-6227; macspeedshop.com; Barbecue/Southern;
$–$$. If you're driving by this restaurant and bar on a sunny day,
expect to feel envious of the crowds gathered around its picnic
tables. After all, they're likely enjoying live music, cold beers, and
some of the city's best 'cue. When the six guys behind the popular
spot launched it, the plan was to create a restaurant for everyone
from bankers to bikers to babies—and they've done just that. With its
casual, cheap fare and large selection of craft brews and drafts, Mac's
has been a huge hit on the Charlotte scene—and beyond. This laid-
back barbecue spot has become a favorite of visiting chefs seeking
a taste of Charlotte, including Anthony Bourdain and Thomas Keller.
A bite of the Big Pig barbecue sandwich with its tender pulled pork
and fresh slaw helps explain the popularity, as does the thick and
meaty Brunswick stew and the crispy onions. Still not convinced?
Order the banana pudding with vanilla wafers and whipped cream and

you'll never just drive by again. Additional locations: 19601 Liverpool Pkwy., Cornelius, NC 28031, (704) 892-3554; 2414 Sandy Porter Rd., Steele Creek, Charlotte, NC 28273, (704) 504-8500.

Midnight Diner, 115 E. Carson Blvd., South End, Charlotte, NC 28202; (980) 207-3541; midnightdinercharlotte.com; Diner; $. Finding a restaurant in Charlotte that is open 24 hours a day, 7 days a week isn't easy. Finding a 3,000-square-foot restaurant that was literally driven down the highway from one location to another would be impossible—if not for this classic stainless-steel diner. Originally built in the town of Kings Mountain more than a decade ago, the diner made the slow trek 42 miles east to Charlotte in 2010. Now, you'll find it serving up traditional diner comfort fare, including hot coffee and cold milk shakes, all day, every day. In true diner form there's a jukebox, black-and-white-tiled floors, bright red accents, and plenty of booths. While there are a variety of lunch and dinner options, including some tasty hot dogs and burgers, and the hand-cut onion rings come out hot and crispy, the all-day breakfast is a favorite here. Decadent options like chicken and waffles, hash browns smothered in cheese, and steak and eggs are popular, but if you've got a hearty appetite, try The Bubba. It's the diner's buttermilk biscuit drenched in creamy sausage gravy and served alongside sausage, cheddar scrambled eggs, and hash browns or grits. Not a bad way to start—or end—the day.

Mr. K.'s Soft Ice Cream, 2107 South Blvd., South End, Charlotte, NC 28203; (704) 375-4318; mrkssofticecream.com; Hamburgers; $. It may not look like much from the outside but this South End dive has been a Charlotte favorite since it opened in The Summer of Love in 1967. It was Theodore Karres who first opened the restaurant (he called it Zesto then and for the first few years it only served ice cream), and while Karres has retired, the hot dog, burger, and ice cream business is still in the family. Today you can step up to the counter to order options like the double cheeseburger hot off the grill and topped with your choice of condiments, or one of the wraps like the overstuffed gyro dripping with cream tzatziki sauce. Hot and fresh fries and onion rings are the perfect accompaniment when you're squeezing into one of the casual restaurant's booths. And, of course, ending with ice cream is practically mandatory. The milk shakes are thick and creamy, while the hand-dipped ice cream comes in creative flavors like Cotton Candy or Black Cherry. But the sweetest treats on the menu can be found under sundaes and parfaits. The famed banana split gives a nostalgic taste of that first, hot '60s summer.

Nikko's Japanese Restaurant & Sushi Bar, 1300 South Blvd., South End, Charlotte, NC 28203; (704) 370-0100; nikkossushibar .net; Japanese/Sushi; $$. Here's the thing about Nikko's: You have to be able to look past the loud, thumping music (there's a DJ there on the weekends) and the amusing, feather-boa-donning owner dancing around the restaurant. As soon as you do that, you'll

realize that this is some of the city's best sushi and it's being served in an über swanky atmosphere with plenty of character. On the weekends it's likely you'll have to wait, but there's plenty of people watching to do here (you saw that line about the dancing owner, right?). So, settle in at the bar for a cocktail and some edamame while you wait for your table. This will give you plenty of time to decide which of the specialty sushi rolls you'll order. Will it be the Alex Roll, a tuna, crab, asparagus, and aioli roll topped with tuna and avocado? Or perhaps the Nikko Roll featuring breaded tuna and cream cheese with masago, tobikko, and wasabi tobikko on top? Or maybe the Charlotte Roll with its tempura white fish, lettuce, and garlic sauce? Whichever rolls you choose, plan on enjoying them alongside some sake while you soak up the scene.

131 Main Restaurant, 1315 East Blvd., Dilworth, Charlotte, NC 28263; (704) 343-0131; 131-main.com; American; $$$. Set on one of Dilworth's busiest corners, this large restaurant caters to a variety of crowds. On weekdays you'll find the dimly lit interior with its high-backed booths filled with those enjoying one of their upscale salads (think delicate crab cakes or perfectly seared ahi tuna) alongside ice teas. The side patio facing East Boulevard's wide sidewalk and offering views of passersby also fills quickly during the lunch hour when the weather is nice. Dinner is this restaurant's bread and butter, when patrons can have their car valet parked from the busy Scott Avenue before entering the elegant, low-lit dining room. Entrees include options from both land and sea, but 131 Main has the preparation of its seafood down to an art. Choices like a grilled trout with herb aioli and chilled quinoa salad or the Cast Iron Scallops, tender buttons of shellfish with lemon butter in a sweet soy glaze, are delightful options. One of the menu's best choices, though, for lunch or dinner, can be found under the casual sandwiches. The house-made veggie burger features a sweet soy glaze and is topped with melted Havarti, lettuce, onions, and tomato on a thick buttery bun. Suddenly, beef looks boring. Additional locations: 9886 Rea Rd., Stonecrest, Charlotte, NC 28277, (704) 544-0131, and 17830 N. Statesville Rd., Cornelius, NC 28031, (704) 896-0131.

Owen's Bagel & Deli, 2041 South Blvd., South End, Charlotte, NC 28203; (704) 333-5385; owensbagelanddeli.com; American; $. You can't help but smile when you walk into this neighborhood, family-friendly bagel deli offering bagels from a Long Island bagel shop. The decor is almost as funky and fun as the menu. Set in a warehouse-like building, the high-ceilinged space includes picnic tables with umbrellas over them, graffiti scrawled across the walls, and eclectic magazine collages behind the register. Families pile in on weekend mornings while the lunch crowd creates a line at the counter that circles around the restaurant many days. Many of the toppings, including hummus, egg salad, chicken salad, and tuna salad, are made on site and bagels come in a variety of flavors and brimming with creative sandwich offerings. Look for amusingly named breakfast choices like the Booty Bagel, featuring peanut butter, banana, honey, and raisin, or Mary's Grubby Bubby topped with egg, Muenster, smoked cheddar, tomato, and avocado. Or, if you're stopping in for a lunch-time bagel, grab the Pig in the Mud, a piled-high sandwich with ham, Swiss cheese, bacon, lettuce, and tomato, or the Tonya Harding Club topped with turkey, ham, bacon, and Colby and swiss cheeses. Between the tasty bagels, free Wi-Fi, and premium coffees, it's no wonder this place is busy just about any time you stop by.

Pewter Rose Bistro, 1820 South Blvd., South End, Charlotte, NC 28203; (704) 332-8149; pewterrose.com; American; $$. This second-story South End bistro is as charming as they come. With its high wood-beam ceilings, hardwood floors, and warm yellow walls, it's instantly cozy. But it's the twinkling white lights strung through tall potted trees, low hanging fans, and the white-tablecloth-covered cafe tables that make this place feel more Parisian than Charlottean. On warm days try to grab a seat on the breezy porch, where you'll find views of the nearby light rail and the other surrounding renovated historic textile mills. A lunch menu features an array of tasty comfort offerings including innovative sandwiches and wraps like the Thai Chicken Wrap featuring julienne veggies, grilled chicken, and chopped peanut sauce in a citrus sauce. And the dinner offerings include dishes like tender glazed short ribs, butternut squash lasagna, and grilled salmon fillet. But it's Pewter Rose's brunch that consistently draws accolades. As with any meal at Pewter Rose, it begins with the light and fluffy warm butterscotch scones, perfect for pairing with a warm mug of coffee. The brunch menu includes soup, sandwiches, and salads, but its breakfast offerings are the star with options like a mashed potato omelet and a creamy shrimp 'n' grits. Enjoy your morning meal alongside one of their sweet mimosas and you can consider your day a success before noon. See Owner Susie Peck and Executive Chef Brent Martin's recipe for **Butterscotch Scones** on p. 242.

Phat Burrito, 1537 Camden Rd., South End, Charlotte, NC 28203; (704) 332-7428; phatburrito.com; Mexican; $. This funky burrito joint is more Southern California than North Carolina. Located in an eclectic stretch of South End, the restaurant's neon yellow and bright blue exterior sets it apart. Walk inside and the look only gets brighter with bold red and lime green walls, colorful checkered tile floors, and a giant chalkboard reading, "Phat, Phresh, Phast, Phunky." Head up to the counter where you can order soft tacos, quesadillas, taco salads, and, of course, burritos. It's a fairly simple selection with the main toppings on each being steak, chicken, veggie, or fish. (Burrito also offers barbecue chicken, beans, or tofu.) The 7-inch-by-3-inch Phat Burrito is your best bet—stuffed with rice, beans, cheese, and your choice of filling, it's a full meal. And these dishes are made, as promised, fast and fresh. You order at the counter and it's immediately created on the grill. If you're coming during the lunch hour—especially during warm weather when the small picnic-style patio is open—expect a line. But also expect to be very satisfied when you leave.

Pio Pio, 1408 East Blvd., Dilworth, Charlotte, NC 28203; (704) 379-1911; piopionc.com; Peruvian; $. If you've ever spent any time in South America, you know that Peruvians have their beans, rice, and chicken down to a culinary art form. Tucked away in a nondescript Dilworth shopping center, you'll find this small restaurant serving some of the best rotisserie chicken and plantains in town. The interior of the family-owned restaurant is surprisingly elegant with white-tableclothed tables, a small stone bar area, and gold-hued walls. Start your meal with the sweet and icy sangria, made on site from a high-quality wine and fresh fruit. The menu features a variety of options including a delicious pan-seared fresh tilapia and a slow-cooked Colombian steak, but the chicken reigns in this restaurant. Farm-fresh and steroid-free, the chickens are rotisserie roasted, making them incredibly tender and juicy. All of the seasoning and sauces are also made in the kitchen here and you can taste the fresh quality in choices like the garlic sauce. Enjoy it alongside the rice and beans, before finishing up your meal with the dense tres leches.

Polka Dot Bake Shop, 1730 East Woodlawn Rd., Dilworth, Charlotte, NC 28209; (704) 523-5001; polkadotbakeshop.com; Bakery; $. Step inside this charming little bakeshop and your mouth will likely be watering before you've closed the door behind you.

A case filled with the day's made-from-scratch choices offers some of the city's best cupcakes, each one seemingly more moist and soft than the last. Topped with irresistibly creamy buttercream  icing, these miniature cakes come in flavors ranging from the complex Bananas Foster, a vanilla bean cupcake with sautéed brown sugar bananas topped with caramel buttercream, to a simple red velvet made with dense, rich cake. Each day offers different flavors, so check the website for the day's offerings—and go on a day that features the Key Lime Pie flavor. These bright and sweet cupcakes may actually be better than their pie namesake. Not in the mood for cupcakes? Polka Dot also offers brownies, challah, cookies, sweet-potato crackers, and muffins—all made from scratch and perfect for indulging your carb craving.

Ru San's, 2440 Park Rd., Dilworth, Charlotte, NC 28203; (704) 374-0008; rusans.com; Japanese/Sushi; $$. When you walk in they yell "Welcome to Ru Sans!" and the service here can be a little slow, but the good—and seriously cheap—sushi more than makes up for it. This Atlanta-based chain may be known best for its lunchtime sushi buffet. For $10.10 per person, the massive buffet features all-you-can-eat sushi and Japanese fare. The buffet typically includes sushi rolls, nigiri, maki, teriyaki, Japanese noodles, fried rice, calamari, salads, soups, and even desserts. It's the kind of thing you'll likely regret (no one should ever feel this full off of light bites of sushi), but if you're seriously craving tons of sushi, there's no better spot to hit in town to get it cheap.

Sauceman's, 228 West Blvd., South End, Charlotte, NC 28203; (704) 333-7070; saucemans.com; Barbecue/Southern; $. When the chef also goes by "pitmaster," you know you're going to have some good barbecue. Here the 'cue is slow smoked for more than 12 hours over hickory and white oak—and you can smell it before you even walk in the door. The menu isn't your typical Carolina barbecue spot though. It features sandwiches, which come in 10 varieties and are offered with your choice of burger meat, pork, chicken, turkey, or veggies. All the choices are served piled high with tasty toppings, but if you don't try the tender, slow-cooked pork, you're missing out. Cut into large chunks of moist meat, and stuffed between buttery slices of Texas Toast, it's a barbecue-lover's dream. Try it on the Sweet Smoke Sandwich, featuring melted cheddar cheese, thin-sliced Granny Smith apples, and house-smoked applewood bacon. Or, for an international-meets-Southern twist, order the Dixie Cuban, topped with pimento cheese and fried pickles. Order your sandwich with a side of the potato salad, which is also smoked and features a creamy texture alongside the smoky flavor. Then wash it all down with an ice cold glass of the house-made Arnold Palmer— just get there early as most days at lunch the drink runs out before the rush is over. Sauceman's is open for lunch and dinner, but it is a must-visit on Friday evenings for dinner when they offer Low Country boils featuring tender racks of ribs in a spicy rub.

Sir Edmund Halley's, 4151 Park Rd., South End, Charlotte, NC 28209; (704) 525-7775; halleyspub.com; Pub, $. Tucked in a practically hidden spot, down an alley and in the basement of a shopping center, this pub offers an eclectic mix of pub grub, pints, and unusual dishes like ostrich meatloaf. The atmosphere, though, is all pub. A dimly lit space features dark wood tables, deep red floors, and a cozy bar with plenty of red-seated stools. Guinness lovers especially flock here for the cold pints of the dark beer, but you'll also find other UK brews on tap including Newcastle Brown Ale, McSorley's Irish Black lager, and Old Speckled Hen. A selection of scotch and Irish whiskeys rounds out the across-the-pond drink list. Sticking to the UK favorites on the menu isn't a bad idea either. There you'll find bangers 'n' mash with peas and sausage gravy, a traditional Irish Guinness stew, classic fish and chips, and surprisingly flavorful Irish potato cakes with a warm herb goat cheese sauce. However, for those interested in a more gourmet—and often vegetarian—experience, Sir Ed's offers unexpected options like butternut squash croquettes with brie fondue, quinoa-stuffed yellow peppers with roasted root vegetables, and a spicy asparagus and portabello grilled-cheese sandwich on sourdough bread. Cheers!

Something Classic Cafe, 1419 East Blvd., Dilworth, Charlotte, NC 28203; (704) 347-3666; somethingclassic.com; American; $. If you're looking for a casual spot to drop in for a salad, sandwich, or bowl of soup, this is your place. It's also the perfect destination if you're searching for an easy spot to pick up dinner on the run. And, if you're on the search for a catering company offering an array of dishes for varying numbers of people, this is a great choice as well. Stopping in for lunch? Try one of the creative sandwiches like the California Smoked Turkey and Avocado Wrap with tomatoes, lettuce, and a creamy cucumber mayo or the hot Brigitte Bardot with ham, melted brie, French mustard, and caramelized onions. If it's the to-go options you're hoping to try, check the calendar on the website for daily specials. The chicken potpie is a homey comfort food, as is creamy, homemade tomato bisque soup, which can be purchased by the pint. And whatever you do, if you happen to be there on a day when they're serving the sweet-potato-ham biscuits, don't leave without them.

Sullivan's Steakhouse, 1928 South Blvd., South End, Charlotte, NC 28203; (704) 335-8228; sullivanssteakhouse.com; Seafood/Steakhouse; $$$. Soak up the live jazz and dig into the USDA Prime Beef at this high-end franchise. The steaks are carefully cooked to order to the extent that your server will likely ask you to cut in as soon as it arrives to ensure it has been prepared to your preference. If you're more in the mood for food from the sea, try the thick and flavorful crab cakes—or, for a real treat, the cold-water Australian lobster tail. Sides are of the a la carte variety and include typical steakhouse options such as creamy spinach or skin-on mashed potatoes. While the food is good, it's the atmosphere that really seems to lure guests into this spot. You'll find live jazz most nights inside a richly decorated dining room with tall windows, dark woodwork, and an impressive wine cellar. If you're hoping to try the menu, but you're not ready for the full-on steakhouse experience, Sullivan's also offers great happy-hour appetizer specials alongside cocktails and an extensive wine list.

Sushi 101, 1730 E. Woodlawn Rd., Dilworth, Charlotte, NC 28209; (704) 672-0990; sushi101charlotte.com; Japanese/Sushi; $$. For more than 10 years, this easygoing sushi spot has been a Charlotte favorite. Tucked away in a strip center just off Woodlawn Road, any seat in the dining room of Sushi 101 feels cozy because of the restaurant's long shape. And just behind the restaurant you'll find one of the city's best-kept secrets when it comes to patios. It's a quiet perch overlooking the busy road below. While the menu includes Japanese teriyakis, noodle bowls, and appetizers like *gyoza* dumplings, lettuce wraps, and fried calamari, the top options fall under the sushi section. Here you'll find large and creative rolls, stuffed with enough fillings that often even just one is plenty for a meal. Try the Ballantyne Roll, a shrimp tempura roll with smoked salmon skin and tempura crunches, and topped with tuna. Or, for a serious calorie splurge, order Sir Justin's Roll, featuring snow crab salad and tempura crunches rolled and then lightly battered and fried before being topped with ahi poki and wasabi mayo.

Thai Taste, 324 East Blvd., Dilworth, Charlotte, NC 28203; (704) 332-0001; thaitastecharlotte.com; Thai; $$. When this Thai restaurant arrived in 1988, it was setting up shop in a city where steakhouses and southern fare were staples and anything other than American food seemed wildly adventurous. It quickly became a neighborhood favorite for those in search of spicy curries and savory stir-fried dishes. The restaurant interior is casual and distinctly Asian themed with wood-paneled walls, red chairs and ceilings, and colorful tablecloths and decor. A hammock is draped across the ceiling in one part of the dining room while Asian art hangs on the walls over tables in another. While the dishes may not be the most authentic or the most upscale, this is a simple, low-key restaurant where you'll always find locals stopping in for a quick, reasonably priced lunch or lingering over a long dinner. Truth be told, the best thing about this small restaurant may be the staff. Those who work here are exceptionally friendly and fast, and if you're looking for a taste of Thailand at a reasonable price served with a smile, you've found it.

300 East, 300 East Blvd., Dilworth, Charlotte, NC 28203; (704) 332-6507; 300east.net; American/Southern; $$$. Set in a renovated, historic Dilworth home, 300 East offers a variety of seating choices from the cozy downstairs bar to the secluded upstairs dining room to the quaint cafe tables on the shady patio. The menu is an eclectic mix of bistro dishes with choices like sweet potato ravioli with a gorgonzola cream sauce or a savory baked French onion soup topped in thick melted provolone and crusty croutons.

While 300 East offers lunch and dinner most days, two of the best ways to enjoy this charming spot are for a glass of wine and snack at the bar, or for Sunday brunch. The wine list is very approachable, with all bottles being offered as glasses and a tasting choice available featuring pours of any three wines on the menu for $10. Enjoy a glass with friends before the dinner crowd arrives, and share appetizers like the house-made pimento cheese or the baked marinated goat cheese with roasted garlic and sun-dried tomatoes. On a gorgeous Sunday morning, there are few prettier places in town than the garden patio of this old home. The  selections are fairly traditional, including eggs Benedict and whole-grain Belgian waffles, but the unique Grits Bowl may your best choice. Creamy cheese grits are topped with choices like avocado, chorizo, fried egg, or fresh chiles. Just don't forget your mimosa.

Toast Cafe, 2400 Park Rd., Dilworth, Charlotte, NC 28203; (704) 215-4166; toastcafeonline.com; American/Breakfast; $$. While the original location of this popular breakfast joint can be found on Davidson's Main Street, a Dilworth outpost was a natural fit for Toast's family-friendly fare. Weekend mornings find the casual dining room packed with convivial kids conversations as the pancake-loving crew piles in for creamy hot chocolates and french toast. And while plenty of parents enjoy indulging in the syrupy flapjacks, there are the more sophisticated options like an avocado omelet made with avocado, bacon, Parmesan, and tomatoes. Fresh-brewed coffee and crispy bacon make it a pre-work casual hot spot, but the lunches and dinners raise the epicurean bar. Dishes like chicken Marsala or pan-seared red snapper topped with lump crab and roasted red pepper attract locals looking for a gourmet emphasis. Don't overlook Toast's spirits menu, which includes sweet martinis like a Dreamsicle of Bailey's, Grand Marnier, and orange juice, as well as coffee cocktails like the Café Toast Café created with Kahlua, Grand Marnier, and coffee. Kids get their special section on the menu, boasting pastas and sandwiches. And the desserts menu features dishes likely to be a favorite of young and old. Banana pudding, anyone?

Vietnam Grille, 5615 South Blvd., South End, Charlotte, NC 28217; (704) 525-2408; Vietnamese; $$. It may not look like much from the exterior with its blue awning, oversized sign, and neon "Open" beckoning you in the door. But inside you'll find a bright and modern interior—and a restaurant serving some of the city's best Vietnamese food. The bun dishes tend to be favorites here with options like a savory grilled pork or the hearty grilled meatballs. Also worth ordering is the pho, which is served with jalapeños, sprouts, and basil on the side so that you can add heat or texture to the steaming soup at your own discretion. And, speaking of your discretion, this place is BYOB. So, whether you prefer to pick up some bottles of Tiger to maintain your Asian cultural voyage, or are in the mood to enjoy a bottle of your favorite wine, you can bring whatever you desire to sip on here.

Zen Asian Fusion, 1716 Kenilworth Ave., Dilworth, Charlotte, NC 28203; (704) 358-9688; zenasianfusion.com; Asian/Spanish; $$. On one of Dilworth's busiest corners, you'll find this Asian-themed restaurant offering tastes from literally all over Asia—and beyond. With its contemporary, dimly lit atmosphere, friendly servers, and pleasant patio overlooking the busy Kenilworth Avenue, it's a favorite for those looking for a drink and shared potstickers post-work or for locals in search of a fast bite at lunch. The menu varies quite a bit, ranging from edamame and sushi to Spanish specialties like paella or empanadas. Some of the best dishes can be found under the noodle section—but don't expect these to be any more culturally focused. A pad thai comes with tender Thai noodles paired with veggies, chicken, shrimp, beef, or even scallops. But you'll also find Mongolian crispy fried noodles, Singapore noodles in a light yellow curry, and Vietnamese noodles served with crispy pork spring rolls. There's no doubt that it's exotic and if you happen to drop in on a Wednesday or Thursday night you'll be treated to live music, often with an international flair. Before you leave, be sure to try the sweet and creamy tres leches cake. Consider it the best—if slightly unorthodox—solution for cooling your mouth from that curry.

Beef & Bottle, 4538 South Blvd., South End, Charlotte, NC 28209; (704) 523-9977; beefandbottle.com; Seafood/Steakhouse; $$. This steak and seafood classic has been around since 1978—and some of the staff has been together since 1958. The owner claims he brought Oysters Rockefeller to Charlotte and you're more likely to hear Nat King Cole over the speakers than anyone else. This is the kind of place where the servers probably know the customers—and their parents. And if you've been more than once you've likely already got a regular order. That order should be those oysters, followed by the New York Strip sautéed in wine sauce with a baked Idaho potato and side salad with a thick and chunky blue cheese dressing. End the meal with a piece of the chocolate cake, a scoop of ice cream, and the feeling of satisfaction that comes from eating in a place that feels like coming home.

Bill Spoon's BBQ, 5524 South Blvd., South End, Charlotte, NC 28217; (704) 525-8865; spoonsbarbecue.com; Barbecue; $. There are two things that you can be certain every North Carolinian will have a strong opinion about: basketball and barbecue. And while Charlotte may not be known for its selection of the smoked, pulled, and chopped meat (we leave that up to towns like Lexington and Shelby), there are a few spots around the city that are serious about their 'cue. Bill Spoon's, which has been serving Eastern North Carolina–style barbecue (read: vinegar-based sauce) since 1963, is

one such spot. Run by the grandson of the orig-
inal owner, the casual, checkered-tableclothed
restaurant cooks the whole hog and serves up
barbecue plates and sandwiches with traditional
sides like baked beans, Brunswick stew, potato salad, or mac and
cheese. Finish off the home-cooking experience with a hot slice of
Grandma's Apple Pie and a scoop of creamy vanilla ice cream.

Pike's Soda Shop, 1930 Camden Rd., South End, Charlotte, NC
28203; (704) 372-0092; pikessodashop.com; American; $$. C'mon
in and pull up a stool at the soda fountain. Order a float or malt
and settle in to enjoy the old-timey atmosphere in this longtime
South End favorite. Sure to conjure feelings of nostalgia for bygone
days, the decor here is old-fashioned pharmacy and tunes played
are 1950s and 1960s hits. The menu includes all the comfort food
favorites you'd expect at a spot like this, from crispy grilled-cheese
sandwiches oozing with creamy cheese to a home-style meatloaf
paired with mashed potatoes and covered in a rich, smooth gravy.
Pike's is most popular during the lunch hour when families fill up
the front patio overlooking the Trolley line and pairs sit along
the inside soda bar. However, when you'll find the real crowds is
at Sunday brunch when Pike's offers an extensive buffet for just
$13.95. On it, you'll find dishes like eggs, bacon, hash brown cas-
serole, eggs Benedict, french toast, and fruit in the early morning
hours and then additions like roast beef, pastas, and soups later in
the day. The most impressive part of the buffet, though, may be the
pastry and dessert section featuring an entire table piled high with

cakes, pies, and ice creams. Although, even with the dessert table, ordering one of the creamy shakes or malts is always going to be the best choice in this casual soda shop.

Price's Chicken Coop, 1614 Camden Rd., South End, Charlotte, NC 28203; (704) 333-2088; priceschickencoop.com; Southern; $. The expression "finger lickin' good" could have originated at this South End fried chicken stand. The chicken choices here are just that delicious. And the setting for fried-chicken eating doesn't get much more casual than the coop. Here, you'll find a counter that is open until 6 p.m. and only accepts cash. While this means you can pick up some of the juicy chicken for lunch, truly the best way to enjoy it is on a sunny day when you can carry it across the street to eat in the grass. There are other options like a fish sandwich, chopped barbecue, and even cheeseburgers, but there's a reason this place has chicken in its name. Order the quarter chicken in white or dark and enjoy with their homemade coleslaw, tater rounds, hush puppies, and fresh roll. Ask for extra napkins and a large sweet tea and then settle in for the city's best picnic.

Specialty Stores, Markets & Producers

Atherton Mill and Market, 2104 South Blvd., South End, Charlotte, NC 28203; facebook.com/athertonmillandmarket. Tucked inside the historic Atherton Mill, this market features local meats and vegetables as well as various works from local artists and purveyors. It's not open daily, so check the Facebook page before your visit to ensure the doors will be open. When it is open, go hungry.

Here you'll find fresh food vendors, happy to provide samples of their wares like flavorful trail mix, spicy pickles, rich cheese, and infused oils and vinegars. Often, food trucks park near the market so if your appetite has been whet, you can always grab a quick bite at one of the trucks in front. Otherwise plan on carrying home plenty of fresh goods from friendly sellers. And if you've got extra room in your bag, pick up a bar of the locally made, fragrant soap or some of the creative jewelry.

The Common Market South End, 1515 S. Tryon St., South End, Charlotte, NC 28205; (704) 332-7782; commonmarket isgood.com. It doesn't get much more neighborhood friendly than this eclectic market where the owner rings up your purchases—and will likely know your name after a visit or two. Common Market fills up fast during the lunch hour with those waiting in line for one of its famed sandwiches (try the Hot Mama—tomato, red onion, red pepper, spinach, Havarti, and mayo all on a grilled hot panini). But this isn't just a sandwich shop. Here you'll find one of the city's most creative beer and wine selections, a deli area offering pre-made choices like a perfectly spicy pimento cheese, and fresh-brewed coffee that brings in locals every morning. And while anyone would feel at ease enjoying a coffee or sandwich on the relaxed patio, Common Market comes with a bit of an edge. First there are the amusing gag gifts for sale like bacon-flavored toothpaste or magnets you wouldn't want your mother to see. And then there are the after-hours weekend events, which range from wine and beer tastings to poetry readings and live music. Common Market is actually anything but common, which is exactly what makes it a favorite in this neighborhood.

Healthy Home Market, 2707 South Blvd., South End, Charlotte, NC 28209; (704) 522-8123; hemarket.com. From the outside this looks like a typical grocery store, headlining a small strip center. But step inside and those in search of organic—and occasionally local—fare are in for a treat. The interior is bright and open with a small, fresh produce area and wide aisles full of organic offerings. You'll find a large bulk section, an impressive selection of beer, and an array of vitamins and supplements. And those with special dietetic needs such as gluten allergies will find plenty of choices here. While truth be told, many of the organic choices can be found in other local stores, Healthy Home is set apart because of its prepared foods section. The market offers freshly made sandwiches, salads, and creative, organic meals like pasta or chicken, perfect for taking home and serving. Before you leave

Spotlight on Coffee Shops

Sure, like any other city these days, Charlotte has its fair share of Starbucks and Caribous, which fill up quickly with those in search of a cup of joe and free Wi-Fi. However, the city also offers a few small, locally owned shops perfect for cozying up with a fresh-brewed cup and soaking up the local vibe.

One of those is **Dilworth Coffee** (1235 East Blvd., Dilworth, Charlotte, NC 28203; 704-358-8003; dilworthcoffee .com). This small coffee shop, tucked in a neighborhood shopping center, offers some of the best coffee in the city. Rich brews in a variety of flavors are offered for self-service, while baristas will create fancier drinks of your choosing behind the counter. Low lighting, casual stools, soft rock music, and the fragrant aroma of fresh coffee give this place an instantly laid-back and cozy vibe.

Another favorite, in a somewhat unexpected location, is the small **Java Passage Espresso Bar** (101 W. Worthington Ave., South End, Charlotte, NC 28203; 704-277-6558; facebook.com/pages/Java-Passage-Espresso-Bar) in the bottom of the South End Design Center. With a pleasant, shady courtyard perfect for sipping drinks on sunny days and a casual interior, this coffee shop serves up good, strong coffee in a low-key atmosphere. It's a perfect spot to grab a cup for a quick business meeting or just pick up your morning latte.

In any coffee shop—yes, even those chains—you're likely to see plenty of locals enjoying a cup. But at neighborhood spots like these, you get the best taste of some really great coffee—and the city.

be sure to try out the make-your-own juice bar where you can get creative with your favorite organic juice creation.

Savory Spice Shop, 2000 South Blvd., South End, Charlotte, NC 28203; (980) 225-5419; savoryspiceshop.com. Regardless of whether you actually need spices, this small South End shop in the historic Atherton Mill is worth a visit. The interior is rustic, but chic, with brick floors, high ceilings, and shelves filled with hard-to-find spices. Of course the first thing you're likely to notice isn't the look at all, but rather the savory scents of the spices. The selection is impressive with choices for international cooks like curries and Far Eastern offerings, as well as twists on the more traditional like truffles in sea salt or varying vanilla bean extracts. And while you'll want to grab plenty for your own kitchen (try the tomato powder or Spanish paprika, or anything from the cinnamon selection), one of the best reasons to stop in to this shop is to pick up unique gifts. With pre-bagged mixtures for soups, rubs, and curries, there's a fantastic selection of choices for housewarming gifts or stocking stuffers. And while most of the offerings are savory (hence the name), the hot cocoa kit is a must-have for those with a sweet tooth.

Vin Master Wine Shop, 2000 South Blvd., South End, Charlotte, NC 28203; (704) 996-7471; thevinmaster.com. So, you've stopped in **Atherton Mill and Market** (p. 88) for your meat and veggies, and you've picked up your spices at **Savory Spice Shop** (above). Now walk next door into this gorgeous wine store to finish off your evening's meal. At this wine shop you'll find overstuffed couches, perfect for sitting as you enjoy a tasting, and racks of fine wines. You'll also find two very cute, small dogs who hang out near the door and a friendly owner, Chris Woodrow, whose knowledge of wine is impeccable. If you already have a wine in mind, that's no problem, but if you're looking for advice on your sipping selection, there's no better spot in town. Tell Woodrow your dinner plans or your tastes and he'll have the perfect bottle picked for you in no time. Want to learn a little about what you're drinking? Check the website for times for one of the frequent tastings and classes with topics like "Sparkling Wines of the World Class." Now there's a subject you could ace.

East Charlotte

Central Avenue, Independence Boulevard, NoDa & Plaza Midwood

One could argue that there's no spot as culturally diverse and historically rich as this area of Charlotte. A drive down Central Avenue takes you through neighborhoods with signs written in languages from around the world. An afternoon in Plaza Midwood offers the chance to stroll through a neighborhood that thrived until the 1950s and has seen a dramatic revitalization since the 1990s. And over in NoDa you'll find an arts-focused community with a nightlife and music scene like nowhere else in town.

The dining finds in each neighborhood reflect their unique cultures. Central Avenue offers dim sum, $1.50 tacos, and authentic *banh mi*—all served by restaurant owners who stay true to their respective country's culinary heritage. In Plaza Midwood you can dig into hot dogs, burgers, and diner-style comfort fare in the kind of places where people have been pulling stools up to the counter for decades. And speaking of pulling up a stool, NoDa's casual pubs are the kind of places where you'll want to find your place at the bar and settle in for awhile.

In fact settling in for awhile is a good idea in general around here. Between the newcomers from around the world and the old-timers behind the counter, there's no place you're more likely to get a good story alongside some great food.

Foodie Faves

Amelie's French Bakery, 2424 N. Davidson St., NoDa, Charlotte, NC 28205; (704) 376-1781; ameliesfrenchbakery.com; Bakery/French; $. This eclectic French bakery is open 24 hours a day, but don't think that means there's ever a slow moment. Set in an old factory building, Amelie's is filled with those in search of a cozy spot for coffee, pastries, and conversation at just about any hour of any day. This would seem especially difficult to do considering its size. The bakery winds its way through various rooms decorated with funky chandeliers and travel posters in a vintage French fashion. Shabby-chic couches and chairs tend to be taken first, but small cafe tables abound as well. And while this is definitely a hangout for the young hipster set and you're likely to find plenty of college-age kids with laptops alongside their lattes, Amelie's seems to draw all ages and types. A peek in the pastry case will give you a good idea why. Packed with sweets from macaroons to brownies (don't leave without trying the salted caramel ones—see recipe on p. 256), it's the answer to any sweet tooth craving. Plus, Amelie's offers savory options as well, including tasty sandwiches and rich soups, all perfect for enjoying in one of the bakery's charming nooks.

Bistro La Bon, 1322 Central Ave., Plaza Midwood, Charlotte, NC 28205; (704) 333-4646; bistrolabon.com; French; $$$. Yes, it's in the same strip center as a Family Dollar. And yes, its name doesn't really mean anything. But don't let appearances fool you when it comes to this Plaza Midwood restaurant. Owner and Chef Majid Amoorpour creates gorgeous dishes with complex flavors. Appetizer highlights include briny-fresh Prince Edward Island Mussels in a saffron cream, a delicate mushroom and artichoke crepe, and tantalizingly succulent seared sea scallops. His honey-ginger-glazed salmon with wasabi whipped potatoes is the perfect combination of savory and sweet, while a duck breast paired with a parsnip puree is expertly prepared. Whatever you do, don't skip dessert. Amoorpour worked previously as a pastry chef in England and Chicago and his dessert dishes reflect his depth of experience with house-made pies and bread puddings. If you must choose just one, indulge in the flourless chocolate cake served with house-made sorbet.

Boudreaux's Louisiana Kitchen, 501 East 36th St., NoDa, Charlotte, NC 28205; (704) 331-9898; boudreauxs.com; Cajun; $$. If you're looking for a taste of the Big Easy, this is your place. Go when there's live jazz music—and you have a craving for beignets.

The menu has all your Cajun food favorites from Gumbo Ya Ya brimming with andouille sausage and chicken, to authentic po' boys stuffed with fried shrimp and served on a freshly toasted baguette. One of the best times to stop in here is for Sunday brunch when Boudreaux's embraces the Deep South tradition of lingering over rich foods and Bloody Marys. Grab a seat on the patio and try the shrimp and tasso omelet topped with creamy hollandaise or the french toast, cooked golden brown and served with a side of baked cinnamon apples.

Brooks Sandwich House, 2710 N. Brevard St., NoDa, Charlotte, NC 28205; (704) 375-7808; Hamburgers; $. It's hard to call this small burger joint hidden, considering its exterior is bright red, but that's exactly how this little gem feels. A gravel parking lot flanks the building where inside you'll find a cash-only counter for ordering breakfast and lunch from an oversized board. The restaurant claims to have the World's Best Burger, and while that's up for debate, there's no doubt this burger, freshly grilled and served in a paper basket, is seriously good—especially when paired with an order of the hot and salty french fries. If you're not in the mood for a burger, try one of the overstuffed hot dogs with the house-made chili. If messiness measures taste on dogs (and it obviously does), then these are off the charts. Just make sure you get there early. Brooks is only open until 2 p.m. and you won't want to miss the chance to indulge this craving.

Cabo Fish Taco, 3201 N. Davidson St., NoDa, Charlotte, NC 28205; (704) 332-8868; cabofishtaco.com; Mexican; $$. All of Charlotte rejoiced when this SoCal-meets-North Carolina spot expanded and added outdoor seating. Notorious for its long wait time, the restaurant is finally an option for those not interested in standing on NoDa's sidewalks for hours. This means that now you can enjoy dishes like the honey wasabi tuna burrito or the Diablo Shrimp Salad much faster. Of course the restaurant's namesake fish tacos should be at the top of your "to try" list. The beer-battered white fish is stuffed in a flour tortilla with fresh cabbage, tomato, avocado, and cheese, and then drizzled in a white cilantro sauce. Order it with a side of Mexi-Slaw (it's topped with pine nuts for a twist on the traditional) and any icy margarita, and you'll almost be able to hear the waves crashing as you eat.

Crepe Cellar, 3116 N. Davidson St., NoDa, Charlotte, NC 28205; (704) 910-6543; crepecellar.com; American/French; $$. If you're looking for crepes, you won't find a better spot in town, but this cozy pub offers much more than the French favorites. First, there are the pesto-brie french fries, a heaping plate of hand-cut and twice-fried fries topped with a house-made pesto and creamy brie cheese. They're the gourmet answer to cheese fries and they're good enough that you'll instantly regret agreeing to split them with your dinner companion. Entrees run the gamut from casual fish and chips to a beef short rib over potato-herb gnocchi in a Cabernet reduction. While savory crepes like the ham and gruyère in a béchamel and maple dijon glaze are tempting, the best way to order a crepe here may be from the dessert menu. The Crepe Suzette, served hot and drenched in a Grand Marnier butter sauce alongside quickly melting vanilla bean ice cream, is a French classic you won't want to skip.

Dish, 1220 Thomas Ave., NoDa, Charlotte, NC 28205; (704) 344-0343; eatatdish.com; Southern; $. Both the atmosphere and the food are as laid back and casual as it comes at this Southern restaurant. There are sandwiches and even a salad selection, but at Dish diners should be taking advantage of the true Southern comfort food offerings like the homemade chicken and dumplings full of thick chunks of dumplings and tender chicken, or the country fried steak served over creamy mashed potatoes and covered in a white pepper gravy. Sides include country cookin' favorites like squash casserole or collard greens and each entree comes with a biscuit and a deviled egg. Leaving here hungry is virtually impossible.

Fern, Flavors from the Garden, 1323 Central Ave., Plaza Midwood, Charlotte, NC 28205; (704) 377-1825; fernflavors.com; American/Vegetarian; $$. Whether you're strictly vegetarian or just enjoy vegetarian dishes, this new restaurant is the city's top spot for dining on creative veggie-focused fare. The small cafe features earthy decor with a rustic mason jar chandelier and a wall of lush, live ferns. The menu reflects this calming atmosphere with an entire chakra-inspired juice menu, as well as an impressive selection of organic wines. Dishes range from a simple vegetable panini on thick slices of charred garlic bread to a sweet potato gnocchi topped in savory curry and cashews. Just be sure to try Chef Alyssa Gorelick's squash blossom hush puppies featuring tender squash blossoms stuffed with vegan mozzarella cheese and then deep fried. Bet you didn't know vegetarian fare could be so decadent—or delicious.

Foskoskies Neighborhood Cafe, 2121 Shamrock Dr., Plaza Midwood, Charlotte, NC 28205; (704) 535-2220; foskoskies.com; American/Southern; $$. This is the neighborhood cafe you wish your neighborhood had. Tucked away in the Shamrock neighborhood, the cafe offers daily food and drink specials featuring farmers' market fare and Southern flavors. Dig into crispy green tomatoes fried in cornmeal, Low Country crab cakes stuffed with lump crabmeat and served with a creamy remoulade sauce, or Southern fried chicken plated alongside a creamy broccoli casserole. And be sure to try one of the desserts—the owner makes them fresh daily from scratch and dishes like the apple butterscotch cake served with warm caramel sauce are one of the reasons the casual bar frequently fills up in this small restaurant. The dessert listings change often, but if you happen to go on a day when they're offering the OMG Coconut Cake, don't even think about leaving without ordering it.

Fuel Pizza Cafe, 1501 Central Ave., Plaza Midwood, Charlotte, NC 28205; (704) 376-3835; fuelpizza.com; Italian; $. This 1930s gas station-turned-pizza-joint is where it all started in 1998 for this popular local chain that has recently expanded beyond Charlotte and into Washington, DC. And sure, these days you can order one of their premium pizzas from just about anywhere in town, but there's no place quite as homey as the original spot in the heart of Plaza Midwood. Inside you'll often find Motown playing and you can finish your meal with one of the $3 Brad's Cupcakes or the doughy cinnamon knots. Or order a slice or a plate of wings and sit at one of the patio's picnic tables while you check out the scene on Central.

Intermezzo, 1427 East 10th St., Plaza Midwood, Charlotte, NC 28204; (704) 347-2626; intermezzopizzeria.com; Italian/Serbian; $$. This simple pizzeria isn't one you'll necessarily hear many people talking about and it's not in the hippest stretch of any neighborhood, but go any night and you're likely to find tables filled with locals who love the pizza and the charm of the laid-back spot. Owned by Serbians the restaurant serves both Italian and Serbian dishes, which seems like an odd combo, but actually works well with dishes like a Burek— flaky dough wrapped around beef and onions—being a menu favorite. If you're in the mood for sampling Serbian fare, try the stuffed cabbage; it's brimming with bacon and beef, and comes in a savory broth.

John's Country Kitchen, 1518 Central Ave., Plaza Midwood, Charlotte, NC 28205; (704) 333-9551; Southern; $. This small diner is family owned, accepts only cash, and is almost always filled with regulars. John Margiotis and his wife, Margaret, opened the place 34 years ago, and these days John's son Jimmy usually mans the grill. While they serve a tasty lunch with Margaret cooking the vegetables, breakfast is the best time to dine at this small spot in the heart of Plaza Midwood. And don't even bother with one of the healthy options like the vegetarian omelet with turkey sausage. This is a place where you should be ordering the fried liver-mush and creamy grits alongside a buttery biscuit. Save the calorie counting for another meal.

Kickstand Burger Bar, 1101 Central Ave., Plaza Midwood, Charlotte, NC 28204; (704) 999-2943; kickstandcharlotte.com; Hamburgers; $. Spend any time in Charlotte and you'll see this is a town that is crazy about its burgers and its beer. So it's no surprise that Kickstand, with its extensive selection of both, quickly became a local favorite. The name is reflected in both the decor—there are bicycles lining the walls on both the exterior and interior of the building—and in the burger names. The Morning Ride Burger comes

topped with a fried egg, bacon, American cheese, and hollandaise sauce all squeezed onto an English muffin and The Fender Bender is served drenched in chili, fried onions, mushrooms, slaw, cheese, and bacon. But perhaps the most unusual and fun burger option is The Hung Over Cyclist, featuring a burger and tomato served between two grilled cheese sandwiches. You'll need a long ride to work this one off.

Krazy Fish, 2501 Central Ave., Plaza Midwood, Charlotte, NC 28205; (704) 332-1004; facebook.com/KrazyFishCharlotte; Asian/ Latin American; $$. Don't expect to be impressed from the outside. This restaurant, set in an old building with a run-down parking lot, is a little too far down Central Avenue to be in the gentrified part of Plaza Midwood. And when you first walk in, the aquatic-themed interior, complete with a giant blond mermaid, is a little overwhelming. But the food here is a fusion of flavors that is so good you'll feel like you've discovered the city's best-kept secret after one bite. If you're in the mood for tacos, the smoky Southern pulled pork version, in a blueberry tamarind chutney, is the South's best answer to Latin-Asian fusion. A ceviche appetizer is tender and citrusy and pairs perfectly with the restaurant's icy hibiscus ginger and honey *agua fresca*. If you're feeling really adventurous, see if Owner K.C. Terry is in the mood to cook up something creative for you. He makes a Chinese twist on pad thai that will have you instantly planning your return to this crazy spot.

Spotlight on Mexico

As Charlotte's population from south of the border grows, so does its selection of truly authentic Mexican fare. And while there are many perks that come from dining at some of these small and often family-run restaurants (think house-made corn tortillas and plenty of spice), quite possibly the top attraction is the low prices for plenty of savory fare.

While Central Avenue spots like **Taqueria La Unica** (2801 Central Ave., Charlotte, NC 28205; 704-347-5115) don't look like much from the outside and there's a good chance your server won't speak fluent English, the homemade salsa selection alone would be reason to come. The tender, spicy shrimp fajitas are just icing on the *torta*.

A little farther out from town you'll find **Cocina Latina** (5135 Albemarle Rd., Charlotte, NC 28205; 704-531-5757), which offers Mexican selections primarily from the state of Hidalgo. And while unusual offerings like lamb tacos and squash-blossom quesadillas may be what lure you in, expect to be among crowds who love the friendly atmosphere and frequent live music.

Loco Lime, 1101 Central Ave., Plaza Midwood, Charlotte NC 28204; (704) 333-7837; locolimecharlotte.com; Mexican; $$. The menu at this casual joint is Mexican-inspired, which means that while you'll find typical Mexican fare like fajitas and quesadillas, you'll also find plenty of unexpected quirks like the addition of portobello mushrooms to many of the mixed vegetable options or the honey citrus cilantro slaw served alongside some of the entrees. However, each meal comes with a bottomless basket of chips and bowl of salsa, and the casual padded booths and sombreros around the bar give this the vibe you've come to expect at local Mexican restaurants. Feeling overwhelmed by the extensive menu? Check out the vegetarian section; specifically, the Veggiechanga. The fried flour tortilla is stuffed with sweet plantains, black beans, rice, cheese, roasted corn relish, portobello mushrooms, and grilled zucchini. It's got a slightly sweet and totally tasty flavor.

Lulu Dine | Wine, 1911 Central Ave., Plaza Midwood, Charlotte, NC 28205; (704) 376-2242; luludinewine.com; French; $$$. If you can only go to one restaurant in Plaza Midwood, make it this one. Set in a cozy bungalow complete with hardwood floors, buttery yellow walls, and a fireplace, Lulu feels like you've just been invited into the convivial home of its French Owner, Fabrice DiNonno. Dinner offers rich French dishes like a braised lamb shank served with a white-bean ragout or a creamy fettuccine a la carbonara with egg fettuccine tossed in a pancetta and cream sauce. If you're going for lunch and the weather is nice, arrive early to snag one of the tables on the shaded brick patio in front. Then order one of the sandwiches like the Back Porch BLT, a Southern version of the traditional complete with apple-wood smoked bacon, pimento cheese, and fried green tomato all on two thick slabs of Texas toast. The best meal by far at Lulu is brunch. That's because while the brunch menu offers many of the sandwiches, including the BLT, it also includes the crème brulée french toast, a vanilla custard–dipped toast topped with warm apples, and the Country Benedict, featuring poached eggs, local sausage, sweet jalapeño relish, and fried green tomatoes topped in hollandaise sauce. Pancakes just got boring.

Machu Picchu, 4715 E. Independence Blvd., Charlotte, NC 28212; (704) 536-1575; Peruvian; $$. As you might have guessed, Charlotte isn't exactly a hub for great Peruvian food. That's why this restaurant is such a find. You're unlikely to go on a night when the dining room doesn't have a few native Peruvians dining on their favorites from back home—and if you show up on a night of a televised Peruvian soccer match, good luck finding a table. The ceviche is a favorite here with its fresh, tender seafood in a light citrus sauce, and the famed Peruvian-style rotisserie chicken (which you'll likely smell as soon as you pull into the parking lot) is fall-off-the-bone tender and expertly seasoned.

Mama's Caribbean Grill, 1504 Central Ave., Plaza Midwood, Charlotte, NC 28205; (704) 375-8414; mamacaribbeangrill.webs .com; Caribbean; $. This casual spot on the busiest stretch of Central Ave. offers a variety of food and entertainment. Some nights—and even some afternoons—you'll find it thumping with loud Caribbean music and crowds lining up the sidewalk outside. Others, it's completely quiet with only the occasional visitor stopping in for a plate of jerk chicken or goat curry. There are a few things that are certain though: The food is authentically Caribbean with most of it having a Jamaican flavor and the servings are always more than enough for even the biggest appetite.

Midwood Smokehouse, 1401 Central Ave., Plaza Midwood, Charlotte, NC 28205; (704) 295-4227; midwoodsmokehouse.com; Barbecue; $. When local restaurateur Frank Scibelli of Big Daddy's Burger Bar and Cantina 1511 fame opened this casual barbecue spot, there was little doubt of its instant success. Scibelli seems to have the Midas touch when it comes to restaurants and North Carolinians love their barbecue. Here, 'cue connoisseurs can indulge in Eastern North Carolina–style vinegar-based pork barbecue, Texas-style brisket, and even half chickens with South Carolina–style mustard. Plus there are plenty of barbecue's favorite sides like red slaw, mac and cheese, and creamed corn. And speaking of required accompaniments to 'cue, the bar offers plenty of beers on tap, including North Carolina craft brews for half price on Monday nights.

Revolution Pizza & Ale House, 3228 N. Davidson St., NoDa, Charlotte, NC 28205; (704) 333-4440; revolutionpizza.com; Italian; $$. Housed in an old home on the busy corner of 36th and North Davidson Sts. in NoDa, this popular pizza spot has become known around town as having one of the city's top beer selections. Even though the dining room and wide porches surrounding the restaurant are spacious and full of tables, this spot can fill up fast on gallery crawl nights, when there's a concert at Neighborhood Theater across the street, or on one of their popular music trivia nights. However, arriving early to wait for a table shouldn't be a problem because it offers the chance to try one of their many beers on draft. The bartenders are knowledgeable and always willing to offer a taste if you're trying to make your choice between local craft brews like a Red Oak Amber lager or a Greenman Porter ale. After all, your hardest decision should be when you're creating your own pizza and deciding over creative toppings like truffle oil, locally raised pulled pork, cracked egg, or house-made mozzarella. You should have enjoyed at least one pint before those tough choices.

Smelly Cat Coffeehouse, 514 East 36th St., NoDa, Charlotte, NC 28205; (704) 374-9656; smellycatcoffee.com; Bakery/Coffee; $. You know those quirky, cozy coffeehouses that seem like they only exist in movies? Well, it's time to check one out in real life. This amusingly named NoDa favorite offers house-baked pastries and muffins alongside fresh-brewed cups in a funky shop playing indie tunes. Colorful chairs, exposed brick walls covered in local art, and twinkling lines strung across the windows give it an eccentric feel, and most days you're likely to find a variety of locals working on laptops or chatting over steaming cups of their frothy hot chocolate or lattes.

Soul Gastrolounge, 1500 Central Ave., Plaza Midwood, Charlotte, NC 28205; (704) 348-1848; soulgastrolounge.com; Sushi/Tapas; $. With DJs spinning nightly, exposed brick walls, dim lighting, and a creative cocktail menu, this second-story Plaza Midwood restaurant draws a hip, young crowd every night of the week. The innovative— and delicious—small plates and sushi are what keep people of all ages and stages returning to Soul. Chef Jason Pound turns out dishes with complex tastes you can't find anywhere else in town. His pork-belly tacos, for example, feature the rich meat cubed in a semisweet Asian glaze and paired with juicy watermelon before being wrapped in soft flour tortillas. Sashimi tuna tacos feature tiny cubes of tender tuna stuffed in a crispy wonton taco, drizzled with a creamy *sriracha* sauce, and served over a smear of guacamole. The sushi is excellent as well and includes unexpected ingredients like jalapeño. It adds a kick of spice and flavor to the Soul Roll, which features slivers of tuna and cucumber. Unfortunately the secret is definitely out about this place and they don't take reservations, so arrive early on the weekends or antici- pate spending some time at a very crowded bar.

Thomas Street Tavern, 1218 Thomas Ave., Plaza Midwood, Charlotte, NC 28205; (704) 376-1622; Pub; $. Truth be told, most people don't come here for the food. They come to catch a game, have a drink, play cornhole or table tennis, or just relax next to the fire pits on the back patio. However, when it comes to good bar food, they have tasty—and generous—staples like pizza, hot dogs, chicken wings, and nachos, in addition to a varied selection of salads and sandwiches. Dishes are served casually (as in, they're often served in plastic or Styrofoam containers), but options like a hot artichoke dip or even a classic burger are perfect for pairing with a cold beer and your favorite tune on the jukebox.

Three Amigos Mexican Grill and Cantina, 2917 Central Ave., Plaza Midwood, Charlotte, NC 28205; (704) 536-1851; threeamigos charlotte.com; Mexican; $. If you're looking for inexpensive, authentic Mexican fare and a lot of it, you won't find a better place in Charlotte. The restaurant is definitely on the casual side with a bright dining area featuring green walls, wooden booths, and televisions often playing soccer matches. But once your food has arrived, you'll barely notice the atmosphere. Hot, crispy chips are served alongside a fresh, house-made pico de gallo salsa, margaritas are citrusy and potent, and flavor-packed entrees come in servings so hearty they're over the edges of the plate. While the tacos and quesadillas are good, the stuffed enchiladas are the stand-outs on this menu. Try the Enchiladas Poblanas, which features three tortillas filled with chicken and topped in a traditional mole sauce with cheese and sour cream. Wash it down with one of the margaritas or a chilled bottle of Dos Equis and your evening getaway to Mexico is complete.

Woodland's, 7128 Albemarle Rd., Charlotte, NC 28227; (704) 569-9193; woodlandsusa.com; Indian/Vegetarian; $$. Before Charlotte's culinary community began to expand its offerings, this Albemarle Road Indian restaurant was one of the few spots in town where you could be certain your vegetarian friends could get their fill. The setting is simple, but it more than makes up for it in complex South Indian dishes like *palak peneer, malia kofta,* and *paneer makhani.* All of the food is vegetarian, but even the most carnivorous of eaters is likely to find something appetizing on this extensive menu. And be sure to order a few orders of garlic naan alongside your meal. It's hot, fluffy, and covered in fragrant garlic.

Zada Jane's, 1601 Central Ave., Plaza Midwood, Charlotte, NC 28205; (704) 332-3663; zadajanes.com; American/Vegetarian; $$. The best time to show up at this charming restaurant is for brunch on the weekends. You'll almost certainly have to wait, but that's half the fun at a spot where the complimentary coffee comes in mismatched mugs and there's shuffleboard out front for playing until a table opens up. The eclectic interior features colorful paintings and photos, with large windows facing Central Ave., while a large side patio fills up fast on warm days. Breakfast offerings get creative with choices like Booker T's East Side Hasher, two frittata-style eggs and sausage served over sweet-potato hash browns and covered in melted cheese and green onions. There are lunch and dinner options, which include an excellent veggie burger, tender braised beef short ribs, and a roasted-wild-mushroom ravioli served with sage butter. But for the true Zada Jane's experience, go when you're in the mood for fresh-brewed coffee and hot hash browns.

Diamond Restaurant, 1901 Commonwealth Ave., Plaza Midwood, Charlotte, NC 28205; (704) 375-8959; diamondcharlotte.com; Diner/ Southern; $. This classic diner had been dishing out meat-and-threes to locals in the neighborhood for decades. Then, in 2010, the guys behind the nearby Penguin restaurant took over the space. Now its menu, featuring burgers, diner food, Greek dishes, and plenty of fried food, draws people from all over town—and beyond. The atmosphere is purposefully casual and kitschy with booths and an almost-always full bar. Most days you'll find groups varying from mom's night out types to young hipsters digging into baskets of fried pickles and sampling the house-made desserts. And as one of the few Queen City locales open 24 hours a day, 7 days a week, this is the kind of casual joint where old-timers from the neighborhood are likely to pull up a stool at the bar almost any time of day.

Landmark Diner, 4429 Central Ave., Charlotte, NC 28205; (704) 532-1153; landmarkrestaurantdiner.com; Diner/Greek; $. Since this family-owned restaurant was featured on The Food Network's *Diners, Drive-ins, and Dives* with Guy Fieri, it has been getting more atten- tion than ever. The casual eatery is authentic as diners come this far south, which probably has something to do with the owners being Greek by way of New York. While the distance from town may seem a little daunting (keep going east on Central Ave.), for those craving a true diner experience complete with oversize portions and decadent house-made desserts, this is your place. If you go later in the day, order one of the hearty potpies stuffed with meats and veggies and wrapped in a flaky crust. And if you're there for breakfast, try the french toast made with challah bread. But whenever you go, don't skip dessert. Baklavas, cream pies, and a homemade tiramisu that frequently sells out make this place a favorite for those with a sweet tooth.

Lupie's Cafe, 2718 Monroe Rd., Charlotte, NC 28205; (704) 374-1232; lupiescafe.com; American/Southern; $. It doesn't get any more laid back than this small restaurant with its walls covered in black-and-white photos of local landmarks and its menu focused on simmering bowls of chili. There are different varieties of chili including Texas (tomato-less and spicy), Cincinnati (sweet and spicy), and vegetarian (fine-ground veggies), and each can be served in a variety of fashions from an oversize chili-slaw burger to poured over spaghetti noodles to simply steaming in a bowl alongside a moist square of cornbread. There are plenty of other options at Lupie's for those not interested in the chili, such as sandwiches, burgers, and vegetable plates, but the focus is chili and one bite of any variety and you'll see why.

The Penguin Drive In, 1921 Commonwealth Ave., Plaza Midwood, Charlotte, NC 28205; (704) 375-1925; penguinrestaurant.com; Hamburgers; $. It's been on The Food Network's *Diners, Drive-ins and*

Dives and on The Travel Channel's *Man vs. Food,* but most important it's been around since 1954. While this neighborhood joint got a renovation and cleanup in 2010, it's still as casual as it comes. Wood-paneled walls and red tables welcome families and crowds in for lunch and dinner. Burgers, sandwiches, and hot dogs are served in paper baskets alongside heaping orders of hot fries and the drive-in's famed fried pickles. Wash it all down with a cold beer and consider this a very tasty Charlotte history lesson.

Specialty Stores, Markets & Producers

The Common Market, 2007 Commonwealth Ave., Plaza Midwood, Charlotte, NC 28205; (704) 334-6209; commonmarketisgood.com. It's small, but this Plaza Midwood market is full of offerings for a wide variety of folks. First, there's the sandwich shop where you'll find some of the tastiest toppings between bread in town. The Hot Mama Panini, a vegetarian option featuring tomato, red onion, red pepper, spinach, Havarti, and mayo pressed and served hot, is a favorite, but consider anything made with their house-made pimento cheese to be a must. You'll likely wait in line at the counter during the busy lunch rush, but these sandwiches are worth it. The next-favored section of the shop is its beer selection. Beer lovers can pick up bottles of local brews and unusual options you're unlikely to find

Spotlight on Vietnam

While Plaza Midwood is home to plenty of hip new restaurants and casual American food, if you continue heading east on Central Ave., you'll start to notice that many of the signs hanging over establishment doors switch to Vietnamese. A large part of the city's Vietnamese population lives in this section of town and it has plenty of popular restaurants to show for it.

For some of the city's most authentic and flavorful Vietnamese food, check out the small **Lang Van** (3019 Shamrock Dr., Charlotte, NC 28215; 704-531-9525; langvanrestaurant.com), where your knowledgeable server will likely have plenty of suggestions for your authentic meal. Just a few miles away is **Ben Thanh** (4900 Central Ave., Charlotte, NC 28205; 704-566-1088; benthanhcharlotte.com), which offers a variety of Vietnamese dishes, perfect for anyone who has a taste for lemongrass from pho novices to experts. If you're searching for best *banh mi* in town, you'll have to stop in at **Le's Sandwiches & Cafe** (4520 N. Tryon St., Charlotte, NC 28213; 704-921-7498) in Asian Corners Mall, which offers an authentic version of the popular sandwich.

In the mood for something sweet? Stop into the small **Thanh Huong Cafe** (3023 Central Ave., Charlotte, NC 28205; 704-568-2940) on Central Ave. for its ice coffee sweetened with condensed milk where most of the customers are from Saigon and the music will almost certainly be Vietnamese. Settle in at any of these spots and you'll get a taste of Charlotte you won't find in any shiny Uptown building. This is where the city is growing and one bite of *banh mi* or spoonful of pho and you'll be happy to promote the expansion.

anywhere else in town. Which brings us to the entertainment side of the market; with wine and beer tastings, as well as live music, this place can be buzzing late into the evening many nights. Whenever you go, expect a laid-back crowd in which tattoos are as common as beer lovers and the music is local and acoustic.

Hillbilly Produce Market, 7024 Independence Blvd., Charlotte, NC 28227; (704) 554-8607; hillbillyproduce.com. This adorable market offers an old-timey feel and all the foods to go along with it. Here you can take a trip down memory lane with salty, fresh, hot boiled peanuts and old-fashioned bottled sodas like Nehi Grape or Hines Root Beer. For the locavores there's an impressive selection of locally sourced goods including locally raised pork and beef, locally grown veggies, and plenty of locally made items from chocolates to baked bread to goat cheese. And, of course, like any good country store you'll find racks of locally made relishes, pickled products, barbecue sauces, jams, and jellies.

Inner Harbor Seafood Market, 3019 Central Ave., Charlotte, NC 28205; (704) 567-0283. Set in an old fast-food building with paint on the windows, this seafood market doesn't look like much from the outside. But inside the bright space offers a wide variety of fresh seafood. You'll find fillets, squid, oysters, clams, shrimp, and even live lobsters. Plus, you choose the manner in which you plan to cook your dish and they'll prepare the fish for it. And, most importantly, the seafood is high quality and fresh every time.

Nova's Bakery, 1511 Central Ave., Charlotte, NC 28205; (704) 333-5566; novasbakery.com. Cute and cozy, this Central Ave. bakery offers coffee, smoothies, and comfortable seating for those who want to enjoy their treats at the bakery. But much of the business here is for shoppers in search of freshly baked goods to bring home. Breads and pastries are baked daily using organic flours and grains to create tasty loaves and sweets. While items like cannolis and brownies tempt from the pastry case later in the day, Nova's is particularly popular during the breakfast hour when warm muffins and sweet breads pair perfectly with hot coffee.

Super G International Food Mart, 7323 E. Independence Blvd., Charlotte, NC 28227; (980) 321-4048. Expect to feel a little overwhelmed—and totally thrilled—the first time you shop in this giant international food mart. This branch of the Greensboro, North Carolina–based chain features more than 50,000 square feet of Middle Eastern, Latin, Asian, and Eastern European foods—all for very reasonable prices. If you're looking for simple-to-prepare options, head to the frozen section where you'll find choices like Japanese dumplings or Indian samosas. Want something a little more creative? Check out the meat cases where you'll find options from cow heads to pig feet for a real culinary adventure.

North Charlotte

Concord, Davidson, Huntersville, Lake Norman & University

Travel north on I-77 or I-85 out of town and you'll find beguiling small towns filled with family-run restaurants, bustling farmers' markets, and friendly people happy to direct you to a taste of their region. Many of the restaurants in this area of town are outposts of those closer to the city, but some of the best food can be found in historic main street spots where the owners know most of the guests by name.

Each area has its own flavor with Concord's devotion to NASCAR bringing options like the elegant Speedway Club with its breathtaking views of race land, and Lake Norman offering plenty of spots where you can listen to the water lapping the shore as you dine.

In recent years it's the small town of Davidson with its prestigious college and historic streets that has drawn some of the most talented chefs. Here you can take a stroll down Main Street, and stop in galleries and shops before digging into dinner at a convivial and cozy restaurant. Just save enough time in your evening for a post-dinner stroll with a scoop from the local ice cream shop. You'll want to soak up and savor all the flavor this charming region has to offer.

Foodie Faves

Alton's Kitchen & Cocktails, 19918 North Cove Rd., Cornelius, NC 28031; (704) 655-2727; altonskitchen.com; American; $$. Seafood dominates the eclectic menu at this airy and elegant restaurant with a traditional shrimp cocktail among the favorite appetizers and entrees ranging from a New England lobster to a Pacific sea bass served with mashed potatoes and sautéed baby spinach. While much of the menu is traditional American, if you're in the mood for Mexican, you'll also find a creamy house-made guacamole served with warm corn tortillas and a West Coast Grilled Fish Taco served alongside green rice. And this is definitely a place where you'll want to save room for dessert—specifically save room for the white-chocolate bread pudding. Melting chunks of white chocolate are nestled in hot doughy bread, and topped with cinnamon and creamy white chocolate. Just try to resist licking your plate.

Amalfi's Pizza 'n' Pasta, 8542 University City Blvd., Charlotte, NC 28213; (704) 547-8651; amalfi-charlotte.com; Italian; $. This friendly, Italian family–owned spot draws college kids from the nearby University of North Carolina at Charlotte as well as local families. Tucked into a small strip mall, it's a casual pizzeria where you'll find heaping plates of hearty pasta, thick overstuffed calzones, and piping hot pizzas. You can smell the garlic from the parking lot, and the buttery garlic knots of bread are the perfect start to your meal. And while the evenings are the best time to go to really enjoy the cozy ambience and friendly servers, if you're looking for a lunch-time bargain, Amalfi's offers deals like Fettuccine Alfredo with a salad and bread for just $5.99 or 2 slices of pizza and drink for $3.99. You and your wallet can leave full.

Dressler's Restaurant, 8630 Lindholm Dr., Huntersville, NC 28078; (704) 987-1779; dresslersmetro.com; American/Seafood; $$$. If you're looking for an elegant dining experience with excellent wine pairings in the Lake Norman area, it's hard to find a better spot than this upscale eatery in Birkdale Village. On a warm night, request a seat on the patio, which offers plenty of people watching—and live music if you're lucky—on Birkdale's central square. But if it's cool expect a cozy interior and menu full of rustic, hearty dishes like grilled pork chops in a bacon-balsamic demi-glace or braised beef short rib with crème fraîche potatoes and a port wine reduction sauce. One of the best ways to enjoy Dressler's, though, may be through its wine selection. With a well-chosen selection of wines by the glass, and an extensive list of bottles, this is a perfect place to stop in for a glass alongside rich appetizers like a smoked salmon carpaccio or the restaurant's famed Thai crispy calamari featuring tender strips of calamari in a Thai peanut glaze with wasabi aioli. Just consider yourself warned that when appetizers are as good as these, you probably won't want to share. See Owner Jon Dressler and Executive Chef Scott Hollingsworth's recipe for **Crab Cakes with Pecan Remoulade** on p. 245.

eeZ Fusion & Sushi, 16925 Birkdale Commons Pkwy., Huntersville, NC 28078; (704) 892-4242; eezfusion.com; Asian/Sushi; $$. The menu is massive at this Birkdale Village sushi spot where you'll definitely want to make reservations if you're planning on coming on a weekend. eeZ fills up with families as well as those looking for a night on the town. However, a wait at the bar does offer the opportunity to indulge in cocktails like the Asian Orchid featuring raspberry sake with raspberry liqueur and pineapple juice, or the Rickshaw, a mix of Cointreau, tequila, cranberry juice, and orange juice. While there are plenty of tasty Japanese fusion entree options, like a shiitake filet mignon or a blackened ahi tuna topped with mango salsa, the real stars of this menu are in the sushi section. The Miss Moffitt's Roll is a favorite, featuring spicy tuna, scallions and crispy tempura flakes all rolled inside and topped with thin slices of fresh avocado and drizzled in sweet eel sauce. It's served with a miniature martini glass full of tuna tartare tossed in a spicy mayo and is a delicious mix of fresh fish and creamy flavors. Looking for something unique? Try Doug's Filet Roll.

It's a Philly Roll topped with thin slices of filet mignon, spicy sauce, and scallions. Surf and turf never looked so good.

Epic Chophouse, 104 S. Main St., Mooresville, NC 28115; (704) 230-1720; epicchophouse.com; Steakhouse; $$$. Either make reservations or be prepared to wait because despite having two stories, this downtown Mooresville steakhouse is always packed. Go more than once and you're likely to see familiar faces—Epic is a favorite for locals in the Lake Norman area who flock here for the tender filet mignon and the creamy lobster bisque. A varied wine list offers everything from $15 bottles to a $175 Dom Perignon, and creative cocktails round out the drink offerings. One of the most interesting parts of Epic is actually the building itself. Until 1888 the site was used by a saloon, which was then torn down to open a dry goods store. Today the steakhouse's kitchen is a room that once housed the feed and seed and the banquet room was once the unpacking and pricing area. If you're lucky, while you're there you'll get a tableside lesson from one of the owners who are happy to share their building's colorful history.

Firebirds Wood Fired Grill, 6801 Northlake Mall Dr., Charlotte, NC 28216; (704) 295-1919; firebirdsrestaurants.com; American/Seafood/Steakhouse; $$. There have been Firebirds in the Charlotte area since 2000 and while the chain is based on the idea of flavors from Colorado, it has been happily adopted by Carolinians. The first

LAKESIDE DINING

If you're in the Lake Norman area and the weather is nice, chances are you're going to want to find a place with a view of the water—and maybe even a boat slip for parking. Lucky for you, there are plenty of options around the 50-square-mile lake.

If you're looking for a casual marina, pull into **J. B. Frogs** in Catawba (7774 Hudson Chapel Rd., Catawba, NC 28609; 828-241-2005; facebook.com/pages/JB-Frogs) for breakfast, lunch, and dinner, as well as a full bar and live music many weekends in the summer. **The Landing Restaurant** (4491 Slanting Bridge Rd., Sherrills Ford, NC 28673; 828-478-5944; lakenormanmotel.net) offers equally casual fare with ribs, pizza, and wings alongside a festive tiki bar. And for a fun twist on your casual dining experience, head to **Jokers Dueling Piano Bar at Queens Landing** (1459 River Hwy., Mooresville, NC 28117; 704-663-2628; queenslanding.com), where you can enjoy wings and pizza with your live entertainment.

Also in Mooresville you can dock at **Vinnie's Sardine Grill & Raw Bar** (643 Williamson Rd., Mooresville, NC 28117; 704-799-2090; vinniesrawbar.com) for their famed crab legs served with their signature cocktail sauce. Or those who prefer to enjoy their views with a cold brew in hand can head to **Moe's Lake Norman Ale House and Marina** (155 Pinnacle Ln., Mooresville, NC 28117; 704-664-1806; lknalehouse.com), which offers more than 275 different beers as well as burgers, sandwiches, and casual appetizers. Whichever one of these casual spots you choose, you can be certain the crowd will be laid back and the views will be gorgeous.

thing you'll notice in the restaurant is its smoky fragrance from its cozy indoor stone fireplace and hardwood flames used in the kitchen. The next thing you'll notice are the hearty portion sizes of dishes like pecan-crusted trout, baby back ribs, and meatloaf served alongside mashed potatoes and green beans. The bar here—as at all local Firebirds locations—fills up on the weekends with 20- and 30-somethings indulging in creative cocktails like the Cucumber Gimlet, a mix of Hendrick's Gin with fresh-squeezed lime juice, cilantro, and cucumber. Stop in for a drink between 3 and 7 p.m. on any weeknight and you can enjoy half-priced appetizers like lobster spinach *queso* or seared ahi tuna alongside it.

FireWater, 8708 JW Clay Blvd., University, Charlotte, NC 28262; (704) 549-0050; firewatercharlotte.com; American/Seafood; $$. This casual, modern restaurant may be tucked away in a fairly non-descript strip mall, but it overlooks a small, peaceful lake, giving its patio a surprisingly elegant ambience. The menu has a large variety of well-prepared—and exquisitely presented—dishes ranging from the more casual meatloaf sliders to the gourmet pan-seared red snapper in a buttery paprika sauce. However, this restaurant's best dishes are those created with its shipped-fresh-that-day tuna. Try the tuna tartare appetizer, which features a trip of tuna concoctions including a wasabi aioli tuna, lemon garlic tuna, and sesame soy mandarin orange tuna. Order it alongside the melon mint martini, gaze over the small lake, and all memories that you're in a suburban shopping center are immediately erased.

Flatiron Kitchen & Taphouse, 215 S. Main St., Davidson, NC 28036; (704) 237-3246; flatirononmain.com; Pub; $$. Housed in a prime Davidson location, on a corner at the end of its bustling Main St., Flatiron's chefs and brewmasters drew not only those from the North Charlotte area, but even downtown Charlotteans into Davidson to check out what was cooking. Turns out, it was some pretty tasty stuff—and some really fun beers. You'll want to check out what they call the "beer tower," a selection of both imports and local craft beers on tap. And beer isn't the only locally sourced item you'll find offered in this casual restaurant. The menu features produce, cheese, and meat from area farms and many of the menu items are seasonally based. Of course, if you're looking for a year-round dish, perfect for pairing with any of those brews, the juicy Taphouse Burger is made with wagyu beef and is ideal for enjoying alongside a cold one.

Galway Hooker Irish Pub, 17044 Kenton Dr., Huntersville, NC 28031; (704) 895-1782; galwayhookerpub.com; Pub; $$. From the outside this traditional Irish pub looks a little out of place. Set in a suburban shopping center, the exterior appears to have been plucked out of the Irish countryside with murals of Ireland, authentic stonework, and Irish flags. In truth it was actually taken off Galway Bay in Ireland. Originally built there, the pub was moved piece-by-piece to North Carolina. Inside you'll find a lively replica of the atmosphere of a true Irish pub and a menu featuring plenty of traditional Irish favorites. For a fun twist on the traditional, try the Irish eggrolls. Stuffed with corned beef, sautéed cabbage, onions, and swiss cheese, they're a great starter alongside a pint of Guinness before you dig into options like shepherd's pie, fish and chips, or bangers 'n' mash.

Gianni's Trattoria, 16 Union St., Concord, NC 28025; (704) 788-0595; giannistrattoria.com; Italian; $$. This quaint Italian eatery was opened in Concord by former New Yorkers who wanted to create an upscale spot offering simple, well-prepared dishes. Gleaming hardwood floors, warm tones, and white tablecloths offer an authentically Italian vibe. The dishes here are large and elegantly plated with fresh ingredients and flavorful combinations. And while there are plenty of typical Italian dishes, there are a few options here you won't find on just any menu. For example, the Melanzane Ripeino features delicate fried eggplant topped with herbed fresh ricotta and studded with sun-dried tomato pesto spaghetti. This baked dish, topped with fresh mozzarella, is about as rich as it gets for a vegetarian option. If the appetizers and entrees have filled you up, skip dessert in favor of one of the restaurant's delicious dessert wines in true Italian fashion. An ice wine or a port is an ideal way to complete this evening trip to Italy.

Il Bosco Ristorante & Bar, 127 Depot St., Davidson, NC 28036; (704) 987-1388; ilboscoristorante.com; Italian; $$. A sleek interior and impressive menu belie the unpretentious nature of this elegant Davidson restaurant. Enjoy a glass of wine and selection of gourmet Italian cheeses with house-baked bread or *arancini* as you wait for your table. Entrees include Italian favorites like chicken breast

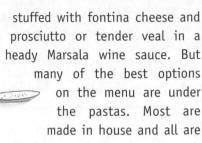

stuffed with fontina cheese and prosciutto or tender veal in a heady Marsala wine sauce. But many of the best options on the menu are under the pastas. Most are made in house and all are cooked perfectly al dente. The butternut squash gnocchi with a hint of nutmeg is a favorite as well as the simple Fettucini alla Bolognese, featuring homemade pasta tossed in a creamy tomato meat sauce. *Buon appetito!*

Mac's Speed Shop, 19601 Liverpool Pkwy., Cornelius, NC 28031; (704) 892-3554; macspeedshop.com; Barbecue/Southern; $–$$. See description on p. 69.

Mai Thai, 3775 Concord Pkwy., Concord, NC 28027; (704) 788-6288; maithaiconcord.com; Thai; $$. It's not always easy finding authentic and delicious ethnic fare in the 'burbs, but Mai Thai is an unexpected exception. The owner, who is from Thailand, has created a menu featuring spicy curries, savory stir fry, delicate pad thai, and fresh basil spring rolls. The Pineapple Fried Rice comes with fragrant jasmine rice, raisins, peas, cashews, corn, and carrots, all stuffed into a sweet pineapple. Sure, you're enjoying this in a strip mall in Concord, but you'd never know it with the dark hardwood floors, red accented walls, and white-tableclothed tables. For the full Thai experience, finish up your meal with the mango and sticky rice. Served with perfectly ripe mango and semisweet rice, it's as good as you'll find this side of Bangkok.

Mickey & Mooch, 9723 Sam Furr Rd., Mooresville, NC 28078; (704) 895-6654; mickeyandmooch.com; American/Steakhouse; $$$. Walk through their signature burnished-brass revolving door, request a booth (they feel secluded and cozy), order a cocktail, enjoy the Big Band tunes, and settle in for what is certain to be a filling meal at this reasonably priced steakhouse. While the steaks here are quite good—they're tender USDA-certified prime cuts prepared to your liking—seafood dishes like crab cakes, tilapia, and fresh scallops can steal the show. The wine list is award winning for good reason and your server is likely to have plenty of suggestions for pairing. Make sure you save room for dessert—specifically, save room for the chocolate cake. It's big enough to split between several people, but enjoying at least a few bits of this moist slice of decadent dessert is a must.

131 Main Restaurant, 17830 N. Statesville Rd., Cornelius, NC 28031; (704) 896-0131; 131-main.com; American; $$. See description on p. 72.

P. F. Chang's China Bistro, 10325 Perimeter Pkwy., Charlotte, NC 28216; (704) 598-1927; pfchangs.com; Chinese; $$$. Sure, it's a chain. But that doesn't mean that Charlotteans don't love this upscale Chinese spot like it's their own. Locals flock to the gourmet Asian fare destination for favorites like its famed chicken lettuce wraps made with wok-seared minced chicken, mushrooms, green onions, and water chestnuts. A large menu filled with offerings ranging from chicken, duck, beef, pork, and lamb to seafood, noodles, and vegetarian offerings means that there's something for everyone—yes, even the smallest members of your group. P. F. Chang's prides itself on its kid's menu, which features kid-friendly Chinese choices like a sweet and sour chicken served with dipping sauce or fried rice made with chicken and eggs. So, bring the whole family—and a large appetite—for this dining experience.

Prickly Pear, 761 N. Main St., Mooresville, NC 28115; (704) 799-0875; prickleypear.net; Mexican; $$. It's not often that you'll find guacamole being served inside a historic church, but that's exactly what's happening at this Mooresville modern Mexican spot. Housed in a brightly colored former Catholic church, the story of the building is half the fun of eating here. Built in this spot in 1944, it contains rafters that are more than 500 years old and made from a tree that is now extinct. And don't come here looking for sombreros or combination plates. With its linen tablecloths, original art, and dishes like filet mignon in a chili guajillo-red bell pepper sauce, this is anything but your typical Tex-Mex joint. While there is an extensive wine list, the cocktails here are perfect for pairing with the house-made chips and fresh guacamole. A sangria is sweet and potent and a blue agave margarita offers flavors of much farther south, but it's the signature Prickly Pear Margarita that's a must for starting your evening in this delicious destination.

Red Rocks Cafe, 8712 Lindholm Dr., Huntersville, NC 28078; (704) 892-9999; redrockscafe.com; American/Seafood; $$$. In the hot summer months around Lake Norman, there may be no better place to see and be seen than this popular restaurant in the center of Birkdale Village. Often frequented by NASCAR stars, the patio here is packed during warm weather with those indulging in the restaurant's extensive menu. The NASCAR scene is actually so prevalent here that you'll notice many of the dishes are named after drivers. In the mood for a rich beef dish? Try Hermie Sadler's Bleu Cheese Filet Medallions, three small filets layered with blue cheese crumbles, portobello mushrooms, garlic mashed potatoes, and crispy fried onions. Looking for something a little lighter? Order Danica Patrick's Salmon, which features a piece of grilled salmon topped with a creamy lemon dill sauce and served with wild rice and green beans. Celebrating something special? Indulge in Kasey Kahne's Lobster Tail Dinner, featuring two lobster tails steamed and served with melted butter. And with live music frequently being played in the courtyard and a lively people-watching scene from your seat, hanging around long enough to spot one of the menu's namesakes shouldn't be a problem.

Restaurant X, 408 S. Main St., Davidson, NC 28036; (704) 892-9369; restaurantx-davidson.com; American; $$$. Owned by a couple from the United Kingdom, this cozy Davidson restaurant (there are barely 20 tables, including the patio) offers an array of simple, delicately flavored dishes. Most of the ingredients here can be sourced to local farms—something that shines through on the flavors in dishes like a warm goat cheese salad with candied pecans. The dishes here are an upscale take on comfort food with options like a pecan-crusted chicken breast in a sage and bacon gravy, and a tender beef brisket served alongside creamy mashed potatoes. And while diners can enjoy the intimate setting inside the small dining room or on the sunny patio in the evenings, this is also a popular lunch spot with its fresh salads and stuffed sandwiches. If you're a fan of British desserts, these are definitely the best in the area with a sticky toffee pudding and a banoffee pie being favorites.

The Speedway Club, 5555 Concord Pkwy., Concord, NC 28027; (704) 455-3216; gospeedwayclub.com; Seafood/Steakhouse; $$$. Sure, you could dine in an Uptown high rise with skyline views or in a lakefront grille with waterfront vistas, but you're unlikely to find a more breathtaking vista in Charlotte than the one from this club overlooking the Charlotte Motor Speedway. While the club fills up to standing room only on race days, it's a perfect spot for NASCAR fans to dine any day. Most of the time the menu features traditional, elegant options like shrimp cocktail, grilled brie, and rich and creamy shrimp and grits. On race days seatings are limited to one hour and are fixed price, often from a buffet. One of the best times to come is lunch, when you'll get bright daytime views of the massive speedway below, where you'll often see activities like driving schools taking place on the massive track. And don't forget to dress nicely and bring your best manners. While NASCAR may have a rep as a casual sport, this club with its white table cloths, wood-paneled walls, and gourmet menu is an upscale addition to the favorite local pastime.

Summit Coffee, 128 S. Main St., Davidson, NC 28036; (704) 895-9090; summitcoffee.com; Coffee; $. Every college town should have a coffee shop like this where old wooden doors off Main St. open into a cozy coffee shop in which you can enjoy freshly brewed cups as well as beer and wine. A menu features plenty of pairings for your drink of choice including sweets like cookies and turnovers, as well as savory fare like quiches and sandwiches. But while the food is good and the coffee is great, it's the ambience that really makes this spot. Look around on the walls and you'll see photos of the Davidson campus, the college's sports teams, and local arts. Most weekend nights you'll find live music, and no matter when you go, you'll experience an eclectic crowd from the nearby school.

Sushi at the Lake, 19732 One Norman Blvd., Cornelius, NC 28031; (704) 987-8080; sushiatthelake.com; Japanese/Sushi; $$. This small restaurant tucked away in a Cornelius strip mall is an odd jumble of Bob Marley music, sports paraphernalia, hibachi grill food, and fresh, expertly prepared sushi. Sure, there are giant images of Jerry Garcia and B. B. King on the walls and yes, the interior feels more bar than restaurant, but the sushi defies all stereotypes. You can watch each piece being made at an L-shaped bar or settle in at a table to order from a large variety of rolls including more than 20 kinds of nigiri. The specialty rolls get creative with options like Kiss Me, featuring tempura crab, cucumber, and snow crab topped with strawberries, wasabi cream, and sweet glaze or the Surf & Turf Roll with tempura tiger shrimp, spicy tuna, cucumber, and filet mignon. If you're feeling really adventurous, order the Sashimi Combination dinner. For $42.50 it includes 20 pieces of delicate, fresh sashimi chosen by the chef.

Tenders Fresh Food, 18341 Statesville Rd., Cornelius, NC 28031; (704) 895-6017; tendersfreshfood.com; American; $$. Sure, the food is served in paper baskets and on red plastic trays. And yes, the white-walled atmosphere with a counter for ordering and posters advertising half-priced milk shakes is distinctly casual. But this isn't your typical fast-food joint. Tenders prides itself on not having a freezer on the facility. This means that your food is as fresh as it comes. The fries are hand cut and prepared daily using whole, fresh potatoes, and the chicken is strictly hormone-free. And while all of that is refreshing in a world full of fast-food fare, one of the more entertaining parts of Tenders comes in its fountain drink machine where you can choose from more than 100 varieties of Coca-Cola sodas. Luckily ordering the food isn't this complicated: Just get the chicken.

Toast Cafe, 101 N. Main St., Davidson, NC 28036; (704) 655-2778; toastcafeonline.com; American/Breakfast; $. Looking for a fast spot to enjoy good coffee, crispy bacon, fresh eggs, and toast with your newspaper before work? Hoping to find an easy place to bring the kids on the weekend for creamy hot chocolates and piled high, thick-cut french toast? Searching for a casual eatery to indulge in gourmet breakfast dishes like an avocado omelet made with avocado, bacon, Parmesan, and tomatoes? You've found it. Not only are various breakfast options available, but Toast offers tasty lunches and dinners as well. In fact, the dinners are surprisingly elegant for a place where kids were digging into syrupy flapjacks only a few hours before. Dinner includes dishes like a pan-seared red snapper topped with lump crab and roasted red pepper and chicken Marsala with a side of garlic mashed potatoes and sautéed spinach. And the kids are invited. An extensive children's menu includes penne pasta with a choice of butter or marinara or something as simple as grilled cheese with chips. And, dessert is one dish all members of the family will be able to agree on with options like chocolate-chip blondies with ice cream and chocolate sauce or a thick and creamy banana pudding with chunks of fresh bananas and vanilla wafers.

Zizi's, 7945 N. Tryon St., University, Charlotte, NC 28262; (704) 595-9170; awesomevegan2go.com; Vegan/Vegetarian; $. There was a time not so long ago when being a vegetarian in barbecue-and-steakhouse-loving Charlotte was difficult and being a vegan was next to impossible. Things have changed and those who prefer their veggies over meat have plenty of options these days with Zizi's being among the best. As the only 100 percent vegan restaurant in the city, it's no surprise that health-conscious diners from around town flock to this take-out and delivery restaurant for its tasty offerings. The names of the menu options here are likely to surprise. Options like chicken nuggets, fish and chips, Philly cheese steak, and spicy Southwest burger are all available, but each is made with meat substitutes consisting of grains and vegetables. Even the menu's sweeter options come in healthy versions with real fruit smoothies in flavors like piña colada made from cream of coconut, pineapple, banana, and soy milk. For those with even more specialized diets, the menu also includes gluten-free and soy-free options.

Landmarks

North Harbor Club, 100 N. Harbor Place Dr., Davidson, NC 28036; (704) 896-5559; northharborclub.com; American; $$$. The food is good at this longtime lakeside establishment, but the number-one reason to come here is the gorgeous setting. Looking over Lake Norman, the interior has a comfortable nautical theme, while the cheerful, shaded patio offers gorgeous views of the water. Boats can dock next to the restaurant and many of the diners come in off the water. While it's a perfect spot for a long and leisurely brunch on the weekends or lunch break during a day on the lake, the best time to stop in here is at sunset when you can watch the skies change as you enjoy one of their signature martinis like the Nassau, featuring light rum, Kahlúa, Baileys, and Grand Marnier. Dinner offers a more upscale experience and while entrees like an herb-roasted salmon or miso-glazed tuna are perfect for enjoying lakeside, many of the best options on the menu can be found under the appetizers. Enjoy a creamy lobster mac and cheese or crisp brie spring roll oozing with the rich cheese and honey-basted grilled peaches. And for the perfect end to the evening, finish up your meal with the Key lime pie or butterscotch crème brulée.

Rusty Rudder, 20210 Henderson Rd., Cornelius, NC 28031; (704) 892-9195; therustyrudder.net; American/Seafood; $$. Don't come here for the food. Come for the gorgeous lake views, cheap beer, and fun casual atmosphere. With live music many nights, this place fills up fast with folks who have been on their boats during the day and are looking for a place to kick back in the evening. So grab a beer and hang out on the deck overlooking the water. If you are hungry, the lakeside spot offers a tasty selection of fish tacos, including one with blackened white fish, a shrimp version, a mahimahi choice, and even a tofu taco featuring pan-fried tofu with Cajun seasoning. Order them with a cold beer and enjoy the scene at one of the lake's top nighttime destinations.

Specialty Stores, Markets & Producers

Derado's Italian Gourmet Market, 8301 Magnolia Estates Dr., Cornelius, NC 28031; (704) 237-3382; derados.com. Lovers of Italian fare can stop in to this gourmet market for freshly prepared breakfast, lunch, or dinner to take home. Mornings offer specialty coffees from around the world, as well as freshly baked breads and pastries made from Italian recipes. Lunchtime features Italian sandwiches like an overflowing meatball Parmesan option featuring thick, juicy meatballs topped in mozzarella cheese and a house-made tomato sauce. But dinner is the best time to stop in this Old World–themed market when you can pick up hearty fare like eggplant Parmesan or homemade lasagna. All offerings can be packaged with a tossed salad, dinner rolls, and freshly grated cheese. And definitely plan on including dessert. The choices are extensive with choices like a creamy tiramisu, tart lemon bars, and traditional cannoli. Dinner is served!

Ferrucci's Old Tyme Italian Market, 20212 Knox Rd., Davidson, NC 28036; (704) 896-3190; ferruccis.com. The interior of this specialty Italian market is not at all what you'd expect in a strip mall just off I-77. Its black-and-white-tiled floors, baskets filled with fresh breads, and shelves stocked full of Italian goods make you feel as if you've just stepped off a Roman side street and into a quaint market. Run by Brooklyn, New York, natives, the store offers

FARMERS' MARKETS & FARMS
IN THE NORTHERN 'BURBS

If you enjoy perusing fresh, seasonal fruits and veggies and checking out the offerings from local farms, you'll find plenty of charming markets in which to browse and buy north of town. The **Mooresville Farmers' Market** (localharvest.org), which is open Wednesday and Saturday in Downtown Mooresville throughout the summer, offers everything from dairy and egg products to fresh herbs and flowers.

In **Huntersville** you'll find the farmers' market on Tuesday and Saturday just east of Town Hall on Main St. offering fare from local farms. The best market in the area, though, may be the **Davidson Farmers' Market** (davidsonfarmersmarket .org). This year-round market includes more than 35 farmers and producers from within 100 miles of the quaint downtown. In addition to fresh produce, herbs, flowers, dairy, and meats, the market offers cooking demos, live music, and samples from vendors. Open Sat until noon.

Of course if you want to bypass the markets entirely, there are many farms in this area offering "pick your own" options such as **Carrigan Farms** in Mooresville (1261 Oak Ridge Farm Hwy., Mooresville, NC 28115; 704-664-1450; carriganfarms.org), where locals head for fresh apples in the early fall, pumpkins in October, strawberries in the spring, and fresh garden veggies throughout the summer. You won't find produce fresher than this—or a more peaceful spot to spend an afternoon picking.

cases full of authentic Italian meats, cheeses, pastas, olives, and side dishes. A deli features traditional Italian sandwiches including paninis and heros all served on crusty Italian bread and made using flavorful meats and cheeses. All dishes can be enjoyed on the patio in front of the market, but most patrons prefer to take their goods with them to bring a taste of Italy home.

The Fresh Market, 20623 Torrence Chapel Rd., Cornelius, NC 28036; (704) 892-8802; thefresh market.com. The scent of fresh coffee greets you at the door of this charming local market. Here you'll find the city's best selection of cuts of meats, a large variety of gorgeous vege-tables, and aisles of gourmet choices. Sushi and prepared foods (try the orzo, pine nut, and spinach salad!) are included in the market offerings as are a variety of fine wines and beers. But much of the charm of The Fresh Market comes from the experience. The door and front area are always brimming with seasonal items from mums and pumpkins in the fall to tulips and daffodils in the spring. Coffee samples come in seasonal flavors—if you spot the pumpkin variety, buy it immediately as it often sells out. And bins around the checkout lines are always filled with seasonal candy—anyone who can resist the peppermint bark must have superhuman powers. The Fresh Market's food is excellent, but it's the experi-ence that sets this one apart from the rest. Additional locations: 4223 Providence Rd., Charlotte, NC 28211, (704) 365-6659; 7625 Pineville Matthews Rd., Charlotte, NC 28226, (704) 541-1882.

Central Charlotte

Elizabeth, Montford, Midtown, Myers Park & SouthPark

Charlotte's Uptown may be home to its big businesses, gleaming skyscrapers, and sports complexes, but the heart of this city is in the tree-lined streets of its charming neighborhoods. Nestled close to the city center, these neighborhoods just south of town offer street after street of beautiful homes, local shops, and top restaurants.

Just outside of downtown you'll find Midtown, a growing neighborhood with shops, restaurants, and a popular greenway offering impressive skyline views. Bordering Midtown is one of the city's most historic districts, Elizabeth. Here, old trolley tracks lead from center city past restaurants, bars, shops, and a college campus to the region's two largest hospitals. Myers Park, which is known for its stately homes facing wide shady streets and its historic churches, offers restaurants ranging from cozy bistros to casual burger joints.

One of the most popular destinations in Charlotte, though, may be the SouthPark neighborhood. In an area that was farmland just a few decades ago, you'll find the region's top shopping mall as well as numerous other shops, cafes, wine bars, and restaurants.

Wherever you end up dining in these friendly neighborhoods, you can be certain you'll be getting a flavor of Charlotte. From the laid-back locals who stop in at their neighborhood favorites, to the stylish crowds enjoying upscale fare at some of the city's most elegant eateries, these neighborhoods offer a peek into the city like none other.

Foodie Faves

Arooji's Wine Room & Ristorante, 720 Governor Morrison St., SouthPark, Charlotte, NC 28226; (704) 366-6610; aroojis.com; Italian; $$$. At first glance the Tuscan decor in this SouthPark restaurant appears a little overwrought. There's the faux stonework and a rotunda-like ceiling alongside shimmering draperies and even a small fireplace. But ultimately the surroundings give the restaurant a feeling of warmth that continues into a menu full of decadent choices. A lobster-stuffed ravioli in cream sauce with wild mushrooms and white truffle oil tops the decadent Italian offerings, while a grilled Chilean sea bass served over fresh artichokes in an extra virgin olive oil offers a taste of lighter fare from the menu. The wine menu features a nice selection of Italian bottles and plenty of offerings for those hoping to simply pull up to the small bar and enjoy a glass alongside an appetizer like a creamy crab and spinach dip with tender chunks of lump crab. Looking for a way to taste, but not ready for the full Italian immersion? Stop by on a Wednesday evening when Arooji's offers a three-wine flight alongside appetizers for $14.95.

Barrington's Restaurant, 7822 Fairview Rd., SouthPark, Charlotte, NC 28226; (704) 364-5755; barringtonsrestaurant.com; American/ Italian; $$$. Since its opening in the fall of 2000, this SouthPark bistro has been known as one of the city's best restaurants. Chef and Owner Bruce Moffett's petite dining room stays packed most nights with locals who flock here for his gourmet fare. The menu, which changes seasonally and includes local produce, is complemented by a small, but impressive wine list designed to perfectly match each culinary offering. And while the dishes do change frequently, there are a few that are worth the trip each time, such as Moffett's seasonal variation of his *foie gras* appetizer. Occasionally accompanied by a blood orange salad and sometimes by a blackberry compote, the dish is always prepared perfectly and offers smooth texture and complex flavors. The pastas are always an excellent choice as they're made in house with offerings like pillowy handmade Parmesan gnocchi tossed in a savory braised veal and porcini mushroom sauce. The best pasta may be the rigatoni, drenched in a creamy sweet Marsala tomato sauce with chunks of Italian sausage and a hint of a spicy flavor. Complete the ideal evening of eating with one of Barrington's house-made desserts like the fruit cobbler, which changes seasonally, but is always buttery and flaky and brimming with sweet, fresh fruit. See Executive Chef and Owner Bruce Moffett's recipe for **Rigatoni Tossed with Italian Sausage** on p. 253.

Brio Tuscan Grille, 4720 Piedmont Row Dr., SouthPark, Charlotte, NC 28210; (704) 571-4214; brioitalian.com; Italian; $$$. This national chain restaurant brings the flavors of Tuscany to SouthPark's Piedmont Row. Generous portions of your favorite Italian fare have made this elegant restaurant a hit across the nation—and town. While the menu does feature more upscale items like beef medallions with shrimp scampi and Gorgonzola-crusted *bistecca,* some of the best items here are the salads and flatbreads. A strawberry balsamic chicken salad features tender pieces of the marinated and grilled meat tossed with grapes, candied pecans, and Gorgonzola cheese in a tangy herb vinaigrette, while a heartier choice, the sliced steak salad comes with tomatoes, Gorgonzola, mushrooms, and candied pecans all tossed in a creamy horseradish dressing and topped with a balsamic glaze. Prefer a few more carbs with your meal? Check out one of the creative flatbreads like the blackened shrimp and chorizo topped with smoked Gouda, basil pesto green onions, and fresh cilantro. Pair it with a chilled glass of wine on the fountain-side patio and complete the full transporting-to-Tuscany experience.

Cafe Monte, 6700 Fairview Rd., SouthPark, Charlotte, NC 28210; (704) 552-1116; cafemonte.net; French; $$. If you're in the mood for Parisian fare, you won't find anywhere better in Mecklenburg County to assuage those cravings for crepes and quiche than this beautiful SouthPark bistro. Inside woven chairs gather around cafe tables in a room decorated with modern French art, old photos, and large mirrors. And before you've even taken a seat at one of those tables, you'll have the chance to peruse the long pastry case displaying ornate sweets and decadent offerings, sure to make you save room for dessert—or simply make a meal of one of the delicate bites and a cup of warm and creamy café au lait. Skip Americanized offerings like the pizzas and head straight to the French fare like a *croque-monsieur* sandwich, savory French onion soup, or shrimp and artichoke crepe. In fact, making an entire meal of crepes is tempting here as they're perfectly prepared and come in both sweet and savory options. Don't leave without trying the Nutella version—a decadent offering with the hot hazelnut chocolate spread oozing from the delicate folds of the crepe.

Carpe Diem, 1535 Elizabeth Ave., Elizabeth, Charlotte, NC 28204; (704) 377-7976; carpediemrestaurant.com; American/French; $$$. This charming Elizabeth restaurant has been around Charlotte since 1989 and just keeps getting better with age. While you'll still find the menu items that have been favorites for years like the warm goat cheese salad with its hazelnut-crusted goat cheese and semisweet apricot jalapeño vinaigrette, you'll also notice that these days much of the menu comes from local farms and seasonal specialties are top sellers. The decor is an elegant Parisian art nouveau, which elevates dishes like a golden buttermilk fried chicken and creamy Yukon mashed potatoes. But there are plenty of dishes that need no help from the decor, like the scallops with a light vanilla essence served atop an almond risotto. All of the desserts here are made from scratch daily and while all are sweet and tasty, none seem quite as down-home good as the peach and raspberry cobbler topped with a scoop of vanilla ice cream.

The Cowfish Sushi Burger Bar, 4310 Sharon Rd., SouthPark, Charlotte, NC 28211; (704) 365-1922; thecowfish.com; Hamburgers/Sushi; $$. If this is the first time you're hearing of the famed Cowfish restaurant, then odds are you're a little skeptical. After all this is a menu that features the unlikely combination of burger and sushi offerings and the even more unusual and amusingly named, Burgushi—a mixture of both. But don't dismiss this concept yet. The menu is huge with an array of tasty burger choices that would rival any strictly-burgers joint in town, as well as a selection of sushi that ranges from simple veggie rolls to creative and complex rolls made with fresh, tender slivers of fish. And the Burgushi? Well, that happens to be ridiculously good. Take the Taste Explosion Roll for example. It features ground beef, applewood bacon, fresh jalapeños, and spicy cream sauce all rolled in white rice and coated with tempura flakes. Each piece is then topped with a slice of marinated tomato and Pepper Jack cheese and then baked. It has all the flavors of your favorite burger with the texture of a tasty sushi roll. Regardless of whether you opt to eat your dinner between a bun or with chopsticks, make sure you finish it up with one of Cowfish's hand-spun milk shakes. The Caramel Chocolate Espresso Malt is so sweet and creamy you'll need a spoon and straw to slurp this one down to the last drop.

Crisp, 1971 E. 7th St., Elizabeth, Charlotte, NC 28204; (704) 333-9515; crispfoods.com; American; $. With its fresh made-to-order salads and sandwiches, this small Elizabeth restaurant fills up fast during the lunch hour. So get in line early to order or call ahead to have your food waiting when you arrive. The salads are the menu's most popular options with choices like an Asian spinach salad topped with marinated chicken, almond slivers, tart slices of mandarin oranges, and crunchy Chinese noodles in a soy ginger dressing. The F.C.N. Salad is perfect for vegetarians with its mix of apples, pears, blue cheese, walnuts, and dried cranberries in a lemon vinaigrette dressing. And there's always the make-your-own option with plenty of choices for packing your salad full of your favorite toppings. For those who prefer sandwiches, choices like the classic BLT with herb aioli round out the menu. Crisp is open for dinner as well and is less crowded then, when you can enjoy a cool glass of the restaurant's house-brewed ice tea on the front patio on warm evenings.

Customshop, 1601 Elizabeth Ave., Elizabeth, Charlotte, NC 28204; (704) 333-3396; customshopfood.com; American/French/Italian; $$$. Go for the bread pudding. If you have no other reason to make the trip, it is imperative that you try this gooey dessert stuffed with apples and walnuts and drenched in a caramel sauce with a side of vanilla ice cream. Don't even think about leaving without it. But you'll want to try all three courses on this creative menu filled with vivid flavors and complex textures. Chef and Owner Trey Wilson has been impressing locals and visitors alike with his cozy restaurant and creative dishes since opening in 2007. So settle in at one of the candlelit tables and order up the melt-in-your-mouth Kobe beef carpaccio seasoned with lemon and celery. Then follow it up with a dish like the airy house-made ricotta gnocchi with a peppery arugula pesto or the perfectly seared yellowfin tuna served alongside butternut squash and shiitake mushrooms. The selective and ever-changing wine list is one of the best in town, so plan on enjoying a bottle from France, California, or Italy as you savor this delicious meal.

Dee Jai Thai, 613 Providence Rd., Myers Park, Charlotte, NC 28207; (704) 333-7793; deejaithai.com; Thai; $$. Just down from the historic Manor Theater, this always-busy Thai restaurant serves up favorites like panang curry, beef satay, and pad thai, as well as a selection of sushi. It's one of the area's easiest—and best—options for take out so you're likely to see quite a few locals popping in to grab dinner on their way home. However, the interior is swanky and modern, featuring softly playing music, a small patio, and friendly servers. It's the kind of reasonably priced place where you'll find guests ranging from a local family out to dinner in jeans sharing a round of the crab Rangoon to dressed-up date-night couples lingering over candlelight. If you're looking for a real bargain, though, the best time to go is for lunch when for $8.99 you can dig into dishes like pad prik, green curry, or spicy basil chicken as well as complimentary soup and salad. Just be prepared for crowds during the lunch hour because the secret is long-since out on this deal.

Del Frisco's Double Eagle Steakhouse and Seafood, 4725 Piedmont Row, SouthPark, Charlotte, NC 28210; (704) 552-5502; delfriscos.com; Seafood/Steakhouse; $$$. Steakhouses have long ruled the dining scene in Charlotte where big bank deals and political bargaining take place in private dining rooms and secluded banquettes. And this grandiose SouthPark staple reigns over all others. Its sweeping staircase, dim lighting, and mahogany accents evoke a feeling of nostalgia for the city's boom days of banking— and dining. Today, though, it's still a spot to see and be seen and most evenings you're likely to catch a glimpse of a local notable at the bar or around one of the upstairs tables. If you're here it's likely for the steak and you can't go wrong with a filet, prime strip, rib eye, or porterhouse. However, don't skip the first course. A steak tartare features a cool mound of tender beef, while a fried calamari is a longtime favorite, served in a spicy-sweet Asian glaze. If you're looking for a way to visit this ultimate steakhouse and not break the bank, head there on a Sunday evening when they offer a chance to dine on three selected courses for $30.

The Fig Tree Restaurant, 1601 E. 7th St., Elizabeth, Charlotte, NC 28204; (704) 332-3322; charlottefigtree.com; American/French/Italian; $$$. While the wide porch is perfect for lingering over wine and a long meal during warm weather, the interior of this Elizabeth restaurant may be the coziest in town for cooler nights. Set in a historic Craftsman bungalow that was built in 1913, the five dining rooms inside offer original working fireplaces including one in the quiet second-story room. If you're making reservations—which you should—request a seat near one of the crackling fires and plan on ordering from the selection of more than 200 bottles of wine as you enjoy an intimate evening in this sophisticated restaurant. The menu is seasonal and while spring and summer offerings feature fresh local veggies and produce, the chef really shows off his chops in the fall with choices like the Apple Beggar's Purse, a puff pastry stuffed with melted Gorgonzola, onions, walnuts, and sautéed apples. You'll also find plenty of comfort entrees like a lamb with a crust of rosemary or grilled elk. And for a sweet end to the evening, cut into the house-made beignets topped with cinnamon *crème anglais* and served alongside coffee gelato.

Georges Brasserie, 4620 Piedmont Row, SouthPark, Charlotte, NC 28210; (980) 219-7409; georgesbrasserie.com; French; $$$.

Named after its owner, Giorgio Bakatsias, this SouthPark brasserie offers a French-inspired menu accompanied by a Parisian-inspired interior. The dining room features white tablecloths, high-back booths, dark-red accents, and walls covered in French photography. In the bar area you'll find small tables and an impressive raw bar with fresh shrimp, oysters, crabs, and clams on ice. And, for the real French cafe experience, request a seat under the awning on the patio overlooking the central courtyard in the Piedmont Row complex. Open for lunch, dinner, and brunch, the menu features offerings inspired from across the pond like a savory ratatouille served over creamy polenta, or a goat cheese and caramelized onion tart with a flaky pastry crust. You'll also find harder-to-find-in-Charlotte dishes like a cassoulet, bouillabaisse, and chicken liver mousse. And in true French form, one of the best options on the dessert menu is the cheese selection, which includes both international and local cheese offering a perfect finish to an authentically European dining experience.

Good Food on Montford, 1701 Montford Dr., Charlotte, NC 28209; (704) 525-0881; goodfoodonmontford.com; American/Tapas; $$$. When Bruce Moffett and his brother Kerry, of Barrington's, branched out and added Good Food to their repertoire, Charlotte foodies rejoiced. The small Montford Rd. restaurant offers some of the best small plates in town with a menu that changes frequently and in a setting that feels as urbane as any in Charlotte. The best way to dine here is by sharing small plates and you'll want to try a lot because Kerry's talent in the kitchen is evident across the menu. But there are a few that you definitely shouldn't miss, such as the five-spice pork belly on a steamed bun that is the Asian answer to the local favorite, barbecue sandwiches. Also worth ordering are the seared scallops in a sweet potato, bacon, and apple-raisin chutney and the crispy quail lettuce wraps with marinated cucumber and Asian pear. While the rest of Montford may have a distinctly fratty vibe, the swanky patio in front of Good Food offers an upscale alternative as a place to end—or begin—the evening enjoying one of the restaurant's creative cocktails like the mint julep, featuring house-smoked bourbon.

Harper's, 6518 Fairview Rd., SouthPark, Charlotte, NC 28210; (704) 366-6688; harpersgroup.com; American; $$. Harper's Restaurant Group has been dishing out tasty fare to Charlotte since 1987. You'll find their restaurants around town including this casual eponymous SouthPark spot that has been a favorite of locals for years. The restaurant offers lunch, dinner, and weekend brunch as well as a popular to-go service you're likely to see many local families using if you stop in on a weeknight. The menu offers a variety of pizzas, burgers, and salads, as well as a well-rounded selection of entrees ranging from a slow-smoked Texas beef brisket to an herb-crusted trout with lemon caper butter. If you're in the mood for something warm and savory, Harper's offers soups daily including a hearty Brunswick stew and a creamy potato cheddar, both perfect for indulging in on a cold day.

Hawthorne's New York Pizza & Bar, 1701 E. 7th St., Elizabeth, Charlotte, NC 28204; (704) 358-9339; hawthornespizza.com; Italian; $$. This casual pizza restaurant is the kind of spot where you might stop in to catch the game and by the time you've left, you know the name of every friendly server in the place. With a variety of brews on tap and specials like $2.50 drafts every Monday, it's easy to see why this pizzeria is one of Charlotte's favorite spots to kick back with a beer and a slice. Not in the mood for pizza? No problem. The menu is an eclectic mix of bar fare and Italian dishes including fried jalapeño poppers, beer-battered onion rings, and homemade potato chips. If your group is leaning toward one of the pies, though, try the specialty Chicken Bacon Ranch Pizza. It's an unusual mix, but the savory ingredients make it an easy crowd pleaser.

La Paz Restaurant and Cantina, 1100 Metropolitan Ave., Midtown, Charlotte, NC 28204; (704) 332-6322; lapazcharlotte.com; Mexican; $$. While its location in the Metropolitan complex may be new, this popular spot has been serving Charlotteans Mexican fare for more than three decades. Previously located in South End (and before that off Providence Rd.), the restaurant has long been known for its friendly staff and fresh cuisine. The new venue may be larger, but the menu still features the same well-prepared dishes that have made it a favorite for so long. Here you'll find a variety of burritos, tacos, and enchiladas, and the kitchen gets creative

Pizza On The Go

Sure, there are plenty of spots around to enjoy a gourmet slice in a chic setting, but if you prefer your pizza from the comfort of your own couch, these are the places to swing by and pick up your favorite pie.

While **Mellow Mushroom Pizza Bakers'** (2820 Selwyn Ave., Charlotte, NC 28209; 704-966-7499; mellowmushroom.com) funky atmosphere and bustling patio offer a refreshing twist from the ordinary, you can order and pick up one of their specialty pizzas with ease. To complete your take-home meal, step into **petit philippe** (2820 Selwyn Ave., Myers Park, Charlotte, NC 28209; 704-332-9910; petitphilippe.com) next door where an expert will be on hand to tell you which bottle of wine will pair best with your pie.

Over at the **Pizza Peel** (4422 Colwick Rd., Cotswold, Charlotte, NC 28211; 704-714-8808; tapandpeel.com), though, while there is a wine selection, it's beer they'll likely suggest for washing down one of their delectable pizzas. Want to know the best way to do this? Order when you arrive, pull up a stool at the bar, and sip on one of the craft brews while you wait. Then, ask the knowledgeable bartender for suggestions for what kind of beer to enjoy alongside your fresh, hot, take-home pizza. Lucky for you, the Harris Teeter across the street also offers a large selection.

For the most gourmet take-out offering in the area, call ahead to **Vivace** (1100 Metropolitan Ave., Midtown, Charlotte, NC 28204; 704-370-7755; vivacecharlotte.com), where the pizzas feature artisanal Italian cheeses melted over 10 inches of thin crust, crisp from the wood-fired ovens. Try the prosciutto de Parma and Gorgonzola version, which comes with a fig puree and peppery arugula. Sound like too much of a splurge? Stop into the next door Trader Joe's to pair the pie with a bottle of one of their reasonably priced wines and consider it even.

with upscale Mexican dishes you're unlikely to find anywhere else in town. Scoop up chipfulls of the tableside guacamole and munch on crispy corn tortillas wrapped around seasoned blue crab with aged Jack cheese, cilantro, and green onions to start. Then move on to the slow-braised pork tamales made with the unusual, but delicious mix of cheddar cheese, raisins, and almonds. Wash it all down with one of the innovative and icy cocktails like the Pineapple Jalapeñorita made with tequila, triple sec, pineapple juice, and a splash of jalapeño juice.

Leroy Fox, 705 S. Sharon Amity Rd., Myers Park, Charlotte, NC 28211; (704) 366-3232; leroyfox.com; Southern; $$. This place is serious about its fried chicken—but you wouldn't know it from the amusingly named parts of the bird, from the Nation leg, breast, and thigh portions to the North breast and wing parts, to the South leg and thigh serving. Chicken is served barbecue grilled or chicken fried (forget the calories and go with the fried—it's crispy outside and tender and moist in). And it's appropriately served with one of the Southern-themed sides like mashed potatoes or black-eyed pea salad. The house-made mac and cheese is a gooey favorite if you're really looking to indulge. Located in what was previously the famed Hotel Charlotte, Leroy Fox's interior is fresh and cozy with white woodwork, leather chairs, exposed brick walls, and Charlotte-centric art. Televisions are lined up behind the bar, offering views for diners throughout the space. Whether you're there for brunch, lunch, or dinner, or just stopping in to catch the game, don't leave without trying the Huntman's Coffee. A mix of coffee, Jameson whiskey, Kahlúa, and Bailey's Irish Crème, the sweet drink comes with a potent kick.

Lulu on the Green, 500 South Kings Dr., Midtown, Charlotte, NC 28204; (704) 332-7537; luludinewine.com/greenway; American/ French; $. If you're looking for the city's ultimate alfresco dining experience, this is it. This small, stone kiosk situated just off Kings Dr. on the greenway offers several small outside tables—and an entire greenway—as its dining room. Opened by the owner of the Plaza Midwood favorite, Lulu Dine | Wine, the restaurant offers breakfast, lunch, and snack options for those on the greenway throughout the day. In the morning walkers taking in the lush paths can order a cup of coffee and bagels or muffins at the small window, while lunch-time guests will likely want to try one of the menu's sandwiches. Many of the choices are the same you'll find at the original Lulu, such as the BLT made with applewood smoked bacon or the decadent *croque-monsieur* topped with warm ham, gruyère cheese, and a creamy béchamel sauce. For those looking for a lighter snack mid-walk, try the fresh fruit or the hummus, then take a break on the sunny patio with its impressive skyline views.

Maharani Indian Cuisine, 901 S. Kings Dr., Midtown, Charlotte, NC 28204; (704) 370-2455; maharaniindiancuisine.com; Indian; $$. The owners are natives of New Delhi and the menu reflects their passion for their homeland's cuisine. If you're craving curry you've come to the right place. The menu offers traditional preparation of dishes like a fragrant *murg takka masala,* with tender chicken grilled in tandoor-cooked cream sauce or *goa* fish curry made with tender fish cubes in a curry of freshly ground herbs and spices. There are also tandoor preparations worth ordering like a *hariyali takkia,* a boneless white chicken marinated in mint, spinach, and yogurt. One of the best times to come is during lunch when Maharini offers a variety of specials including a curry lunch with lamb curry, basmati rice, and naan bread. There's also a lunch buffet for just $8.25 on which you can indulge in unlimited quantities of the slow-cooked, savory dishes.

Mama Ricotta's Restaurant, 601 S. Kings Dr., Midtown, Charlotte, NC 28204; (704) 343-0148; mamaricottasrestaurant .com; Italian; $$$. You can smell the garlic from the parking lot at this family-friendly Italian spot in Midtown—and that's a good thing. Because it's coming from the restaurant's freshly baked and complimentary buttery rolls. The spacious dining room (it seats 90) features gold walls and shelves brimming with tins of tomatoes. While the menu offers a variety of pizzas, salads, and entrees, it's the pastas that reign supreme in this Italian spot—specifically, the penne a la vodka. This al dente penne pasta, tossed with sautéed pancetta in a peppery vodka and spicy tomato cream sauce, is a consistent favorite for good reason. It's velvety and decadent and when topped with the grilled chicken, makes a hearty meal. In fact all meals at Mama Ricotta's will likely be quite filling. Most dishes come in family-size portions, which gives you a chance to pass heaping bowls of steaming pasta like the rigatoni with meat sauce or penne, broccoli, and chicken, around the table. You'll probably be too full for dessert, but if you happened to have saved room, the panna cotta is a perfectly wobbly version of the baked cream, topped with a sweet, sticky strawberry sauce.

Mellow Mushroom Pizza Bakers, 2820 Selwyn Ave., Myers Park, Charlotte, NC 28209; (704) 966-7499; mellowmushroom.com/myerspark; Italian; $$. It doesn't get much more playful than a pizza joint with a giant school bus parked inside. The colorful interior of this boisterous restaurant hints at its menu, which is dedicated to all things pizza and beer. The salads and munchies are tasty, but plan on ordering them alongside one of the crispy, specialty pies. And while traditional options are available, Mellow Mushroom's best pizzas are their amusingly named innovative choices like the Kosmic Karma topped with red sauce, mozzarella, sun-dried tomatoes, spinach, feta, and pesto, or the Funky Q Chicken with its barbecue chicken, mozzarella, cheddar, caramelized onions, applewood smoked bacon, and barbecue sauce. Quite possibly, though, the most unusual and tasty pizza to enjoy while checking out the modern-hippie restaurant's wall-long photo of Woodstock is the Red Skin Potato Pie. With an olive oil and garlic base, the pizza is piled high with red potatoes, applewood smoked bacon, caramelized onions, cheddar, and mozzarella cheese before being topped with chives, sour cream, and spicy ranch dressing. It may demand a diet immediately following finishing, but it's worth every creamy calorie. Additional location: 14835 Ballantyne Village Way, Ballantyne, Charlotte, NC 28277; (704) 369-5300.

The Melting Pot, 901 S. Kings Dr., Midtown, Charlotte, NC 28204; (704) 334-4400; meltingpot.com; American/Fondue; $$$. It may have been a while since the heyday of fondue, but this restaurant chain still has 145 locations across the US because when it comes to fine dining-meets-dipping, no one does it better. By now you likely know the drill. Each dinner is centered around a fondue pot in which you'll dip everything from bread to apples to meat all in a romantic and elegant setting. Your best bet here is to indulge in the "Big Night Out" four-course dinner, offering a cheese fondue, a fresh seasonal salad (no dipping included), an entree such as steak or chicken accompanied by homemade dipping sauces, and a chocolate fondue dessert. And if you're interested in a slightly smaller version of a fondue evening, just stop in for the chocolate. All of the melted offerings are silky and decadent, but none makes for a sweeter end to the evening than the Flaming Turtle, a mix of milk chocolate, caramel, and candied pecans.

Meskerem Ethiopian Cuisine, 601 S. Kings Dr., Midtown, Charlotte, NC 28204; (704) 335-1197; meskeremincharlotte.com; Ethiopian; $$. Get ready to eat great food—with your hands. There are no utensils at this small, casual Ethiopian spot in a Midtown strip mall. You'll strictly use the *injera* bread to sop up all the savory flavors of these dishes. Before you bother with the entrees, order the avocado salad. This chopped avocado dish features the creamy fruit mixed with diced tomatoes, green peppers, and onions served alongside the bread. The serving is huge, can easily be split, and is more avocado for $6.25 than you'll find anywhere else in town.

The Doro Wat entree, featuring tender pieces of chicken seasoned with onions, garlic, and fresh ginger, is a hearty dish and worth getting your fingers messy. For novices of Ethiopian cuisine, there are plenty of culinary surprises here like the hard-boiled egg served alongside the Doro Wat or the unusual spongy texture of the bread. But the owners, who are from Ethiopia, are friendly and helpful, and you'll find that you'll soon be craving this country's unique cuisine.

Mezzanotte, 2907 Providence Rd., Myers Park, Charlotte, NC 28211; (704) 365-4650; contesrestaurantgroup.com; Italian; $$. Known for its brick-oven pizzas, this cozy Italian spot features large wooden tables with views of your pie being prepared. While there are salads, pastas, and paninis on the menu, this is the kind of spot where pizza should be mandatory. The eponymously named Mezzanotte Pizza, not surprisingly, is one of the best on the menu. Topped with plenty of fresh mozzarella, chunks of tender mush-rooms, and rich sausage, this pizza is the kind of thing you'll return for repeatedly once you've tasted it. However, another top pizza option is actually meatless. The vegetarian pizza is piled high with smoked mozzarella, basil, and a multitude of fresh grilled veggies.

The choice here should not be if, but rather when, you go. And the answer is on a Wednesday when they offer half-price bottles of wine to pair with your pie.

Mueller's Neighborhood Grill, 119 Huntley Pl., Myers Park, Charlotte, NC 28207; (704) 940-6880; muellersgrill.com; Hamburgers; $. Tucked away in the unexpected corner of a parking lot just off the busy intersection of Providence and Queens, this casual burger joint used to be the city's best-kept secret. But these days the secret is out and crowds line up at the grill for the juicy burgers served up fresh from the grill. These are messy burgers for which you'll need both hands and plenty of napkins to enjoy. There are other offerings on the menu including grilled chicken and hot dogs, and while they're good, the burgers tend to steal the show. The interior is a no-frills kind of spot where you call your order over the grill and pay at the counter making the patio, which is more of an extension of the parking lot, your best bet for dining on sunny days.

1900 Mexican Grill, 1523 Elizabeth Ave., Elizabeth, Charlotte, NC 28204; (704) 334-4677; 1900mexicangrill.com; Mexican; $$. If you're looking for a margarita fix with a side of fajitas, this is your place. Settle in to a table at this Elizabeth location of the local restaurant (there's another location in SouthPark) and enjoy a basket of fresh tortilla chips and tomato salsa while you decide between options like tender chicken enchiladas, fried pork carnitas, or chiles rellenos—or from a large selection of tacos and burritos. The SouthPark location tends to be more on the casual side with tables filled with families and friends catching the game over a bowl of the house-made guacamole. But this Elizabeth version is a little more on the upscale end with its open and airy interior and popular bar where you'll find drink specials many nights. Dos Equis anyone?

Nolen Kitchen, 2839 Selwyn Ave., Myers Park, Charlotte, NC 28209; (704) 372-1424; nolenkitchen.com; American/Greek; $$$. There may not be a patio in town as popular as the one at this Myers Park restaurant. With white lights strung above it and frequent live music, this alfresco spot has long been a neighborhood favorite. Of course the fact that the restaurant is serving an eclectic mix of gourmet American fare and Greek-influenced dishes doesn't hurt with drawing the crowds either. Appetizers like pork-belly tacos and risotto fritters sprinkled in Parmesan are perfect for pairing with one of the restaurant's frequent wine specials. The entrees are split into surf and turf with seafood options like a glazed salmon served alongside shiitake risotto and tasty meat choices like a slow-braised short rib in a hoisin glaze accompanied by jalapeño corn pudding. It's an upscale clientele here most nights and you'll find the bar packed with 20- and 30-somethings, especially on Thursday evenings when live music and drink specials always draw a crowd.

Paco's Tacos & Tequila, 6401 Morrison Blvd., SouthPark, Charlotte, NC 28211; (704) 716-8226; pacostacosandtequila.com; Mexican; $$. SouthPark got serious about Tex Mex—and tequila—with the arrival of this upscale Mexican restaurant. The interior features shimmering metal behind the bar, vintage ads, rustic light fixtures that appear to be simply hanging bulbs, and colorful Mexican accents. A patio outside offers seating for 20, while the spacious interior can seat up to 200. Come to Paco's hungry—and thirsty. You'll want to taste from the selection of more than 60 different kinds of tequila that range from luxurious Anejos designed for sipping to others that are perfect for mixing in your favorite specialty margarita made with fresh fruit juices. When it comes to food, the menu is equally extensive with soups, salads, enchiladas, quesadillas, fajitas, and even a chili cheeseburger. But follow the name and go with the tacos. You can mix and match them and choose your preferred shell—flour, corn, or crispy. While they range from barbecue shrimp and red river fish to gringo beef and wood-grilled chicken, the best by far is the Paco's Taco. It's tender brisket mixed with caramelized onions and topped with chipotle barbecue sauce and white cheese. If you're of the vegetarian persuasion, the veggie taco offers a twist on the ordinary with white cheese, cilantro, cabbage, roasted peppers, pickled onions, and chipotle ranch. Order it alongside the table-side guacamole and one of the fresh-fruit margaritas and you may have the most flavorful vegetarian meal in town. See Owner Frank Scibelli's recipe for **Chicken Tortilla Soup** on p. 248.

The Palm Restaurant, 6705 Phillips Place Ct., SouthPark, Charlotte, NC 28210; (704) 552-7256; thepalm.com; Seafood/ Steakhouse; $$$. This elegant, white-tableclothed steakhouse is one of the more attractive spots for dining in town. Large windows offer plenty of light and a long bar is perfect for enjoying a cocktail and one of the restaurant's traditional appetizers. This is the kind of place where the servings are so huge, your steak is likely to actually hang off the plate—and yes, in case you were wondering, ordering steak is practically mandatory. Other things that are must-orders include the jumbo shrimp cocktail with three plump, chilled shrimp presented in an "atomic" cocktail sauce that appears to be smoking. And finally, don't skip dessert. One slice of the flourless chocolate cake made with dark bittersweet chocolate is rich and sweet enough to satisfy any chocolate cravings indefinitely.

Pisces Sushi Bar and Lounge, 1100 E. Metropolitan Ave., Midtown, Charlotte, NC 28204; (704) 334-0009; piscessushi.com; Japanese/Sushi; $$. Located in the Metropolitan complex, this sushi bar features high ceilings, modern design, and bright colors. A small side room offers private, tucked-away booths, while the main dining room is lively and full most evenings. While the evenings are a good time to go, when you can indulge in one of their many sakes, upscale dishes like a honey-glazed duck breast, and desserts like a sweet and creamy green tea ice cream, the best time for Pisces is weekday lunch. From 11:30 a.m. to 2:30 p.m. Monday through Friday, this sushi spot offers what may be the best lunch deal in town. During this time, for $11.95, you can enjoy all-you-can-eat fresh-made sushi. This isn't buffet style—diners place orders with a server who brings out heaping platters of sushi. And then you order again. And again. Until you've had your fill of options like the spicy tuna roll, the Philly roll, the eel and avocado roll, or the shrimp tempura roll, among many others. Garlic noodles, vegetable spring rolls, and rice round out the all-you-can-eat options. Just make sure you go early—Pisces fills up fast and once you've tasted this sushi, you'll understand why.

The Pizza Peel and Tap Room, 4422 Colwick Rd., Cotswold, Charlotte, NC 28211; (704) 714-8808; tapandpeel.com; Italian; $$. If you like craft beer and you enjoy a good slice of pizza, you won't go wrong at this cozy and casual Cotswold restaurant. With more than 40 beers on tap and pizzas made with an airy and sweet wheat crust, it's no wonder this warm tavern-esque spot fills up early most evenings. The rustic interior is much of the charm here with wooden pizza peels hanging on the walls, and chalkboards declaring the day's specials. Settle in at the bar to catch a game with your beer on one of the two large televisions, or bring the family and share a pizza or two in one of the booths along the wall. Specialty pizzas like the Sorry for Partying Supreme are unapologetically heavy on the good stuff with sausage, ground beef, mozzarella cheese, peppers, onions, and mushrooms piled high on top. And for one of the best lunch deals in the neighborhood, stop in on weekdays for the lunch buffet, which offers all-you-can-eat pizza along with a salad and drink for just $7.50.

Roasting Company, 1601 Montford Dr., Charlotte, NC 28209; (704) 521-8188; roastingco.com; American; $. At this casual, order-at-the-counter restaurant on Montford Dr., the fragrance of roasting chicken wafts out the door as you enter. The bird is served in a variety of ways here, from rotisserie chicken dinners to chicken and black bean combos, wraps, salads, sandwiches, and even tacos. But the best way to get your chicken fix here is with the chicken potpie. It's only served on Wednesday, and the pie has a devoted following who show up early to purchase the dish. One bite of the peppery concoction featuring shredded meat, potatoes, peas, and onions, and you'll see why. For an easy at-home meal, order it to go and then just try to resist it until dinnertime.

Rooster's Wood-Fired Kitchen, 6601 Morrison Blvd., SouthPark, Charlotte, NC 28211; (704) 366-8688; roosterskitchen.com; Southern; $$$. See description on p. 38.

Smalls, 1609 Elizabeth Ave., Elizabeth, Charlotte, NC 28204; (704) 334-8338; smallscharlotte.com; American/Hamburgers; $$. Next door to Elizabeth's popular Visulite theater, this is the kind of restaurant you'll immediately want to share with your out-of-town friends. After all you'll want to show off the joint that serves only North Carolina beers, offers a cheeseburger topped with pimento cheese and fried pickles, and offers a chicken and waffles that many claim are the best in the city. It's a bright and boldly decorated spot that feels as eclectic as its menu, which includes everything from fried pickles to sea scallops on a vegetable puree. But back to those chicken and waffles. The chicken is crispy, the waffles are

THE CITY'S BEST PATIOS

With its breezy springs, warm summers, crisp falls, and mild winters, Charlotte is a city where patios fill up fast most of the year. And while many of the restaurants around town offer some form of outside seating, there are a few that stand apart from the rest. Some of the top patios in central Charlotte can actually be found at neighborhood bars where locals are often soaking up the sun with a drink in hand many afternoons.

If you prefer your alfresco cocktail with a skyline view, stop in to **Loft 1523** (1523 Elizabeth Ave., Elizabeth, Charlotte, NC 28204; 704-333-5898; loft1523.com) in Elizabeth. The bar's second-story patio offers some of the city's best views of the nearby skyline. Modern white and blue furniture offers sophisticated seating to match drinks with names like The Elitist Martini, a mix of Stoli Elite with olives, or the Sidecar1523, a traditional mix of Bacardi silver, brandy, lime juice, and triple sec.

made with thyme, and the whole thing is topped in a salted caramel butter that is almost cloyingly sweet. They're the restaurant's best-seller for a reason. Head there in the evenings Wednesday through Saturday to catch live music from local bands—and enjoy one of those NC craft brews.

Sunflour Baking Company, 2001 E. 7th St., Elizabeth, Charlotte, NC 28204; (704) 900-5268; sunflourbakingcompany.com; Bakery; $. Stepping in to this sweet-smelling bakery is proof enough that

For a more laid-back patio, head to Myers Park's **Selwyn Pub** (2801 Selwyn Ave., Myers Park, Charlotte, NC 28209; 704-333-3443; facebook.com/pages/Selwyn-Avenue-Pub), a longtime Charlotte favorite where the tree-shaded deck gets packed early year round. The spring and summer draw out preppy crowds in pastels enjoying buckets of cold beers in the cool shade, while in the fall you're lucky to find a seat with a view of one of the large screens showing ACC and SEC football on the field. Even on mild winter nights, the patio fills fast with revelers sitting around the cozy fire and splitting an order of pizza or wings.

If you're looking for a relaxed alfresco experience, stop by **Brazwell's** (1627 Montford Dr., Charlotte, NC 28209; 704-523-3500; brazwellspub.com) on Montford Dr. for lunch. With oak trees shading the porch and deck and a decent selection of burgers and fries, it's a good spot to stop in for a casual bite and drink. And if you're looking for a place to mingle with crowds over your drinks, stop by later in the evening during warm weather when this patio becomes a hotspot for 20-somethings seeking cheap beer and a good time.

you're in for a treat. Each morning Sunflour offers made-from-scratch croissants, breads, and pastries, all for sale in their cozy, bright bakery. For the day's latest treats, check the chalkboard or take a peek in the pastry case, which is always brimming with fluffy muffins, flaky croissants, and decadent pastries like maca-roons, pies, and cupcakes (try the Key lime ones!). And while the sweets are certainly tempting, the breakfast and lunch menus go far beyond sugary offerings with creamy café au laits offered along-side savory options like a ham and gruyère croissant or a sweet hazelnut orange roll for breakfast, or lunch choices like freshly made quiche or an herbed egg salad sandwich. Interested in special ordering your dessert ahead? Sunflour offers a variety of luscious 9-inch pies like a banana cream pie coated with dark chocolate and pastry cream or a Key lime version made with lime juice sent directly from Key West. It's a good thing these pies are available for take out because licking your plate—which you'll inevitably be tempted to do—is much less embarrassing at home.

Table 274, 274 S. Sharon Amity Rd., Cotswold, Charlotte, NC 28211; (704) 817-9721; table274.com; American; $$$. If you have a chance while you're here, take a peek in the kitchen. This Cotswold restaurant with its clean, modern design and Carolina-grown focused menu, is dedicated to constructing complex dishes from scratch on site. Take the beet ravioli, for example, a deep red ravioli with carrot ricotta that is unexpectedly savory in flavor. Charcuteries, soups, and stocks also get their start in this kitchen, which offers a variety of small and large plates. And if you're looking for a spot to take a group with varied tastes, this is it. The menu ranges from a bacon cheeseburger served with hot, crispy fries to a bowl of rosemary pappardelle tossed with roasted wild mushrooms in a white truffle sauce. Regardless of what you're in the mood for, this is an easy spot to venture to most evenings as its large dining room and secluded location mean you're likely to get your choice of tables on either the quiet patio or in the sleek interior.

Taco Mac, 4625 Piedmont Row Dr., SouthPark, Charlotte, NC 28210; (704) 972-0503; tacomac.com; American/Mexican; $. This large Atlanta-based sports bar has two claims to fame: its beer selection (there are 140 on tap, plus 250 bottled options) and its televisions (there are more than 75 and one of them is a 103-inch plasma hung over the bar). However, if this wasn't enough to sell you on this being the next place you want to watch the big game, consider the menu. While it has a somewhat Southwestern slant—hence the name—the selection here is huge and varied. You can chow down on a variety of sandwiches from a Reuben to a Philly, and enjoy burgers, salads, and soups as well. But the tacos are tasty, as are the quesadillas, burritos, and fajitas, all of which go quite well with one of those 300-plus beer options. If you're just there looking for bar food to pair with your game watching, try the loaded sweet potato fries. Topped with crumbled blue cheese, scallions, tomatoes, and crispy bacon with a side of blue cheese dressing, these are the kind of thing your cardiologist will wish you'd never discovered—but you'll be thrilled you did.

10 at Park Lanes, 1700 Montford Dr., Charlotte, NC 28209; (704) 523-7633; rollten.com; Southern; $$. Bowling fans may have been disappointed when the retro George Pappas Park Lanes closed. But food fans were thrilled when this comfort-food-serving restaurant opened in its place—and still paid homage to its playful past. Here you'll find several outdoor patios, including a beer garden with more than 20 beers on tap, as well as games like cornhole, bocce, and table tennis. The menu has fun, too, with options like Mason

Jar Stacks, featuring the classic jars stacked with choices like prime rib, mac and cheese, and smoked jalapeños. The bar here may be the most creative spot with a dispensing system that appears similar to that of a still. But don't worry—your hooch comes in custom cocktails like the Moonswine Mary, a spicy moonshine-meets-Bloody-Mary mix featuring jalapeño- and bacon-infused moonshine.

Terrace Cafe, 4625 Piedmont Row Dr., SouthPark, Charlotte, NC 28210; (704) 554-6177; terracecafecharlotte.com; American; $$$. The first thing you need to know about this SouthPark restaurant is that they serve red velvet waffles with cream cheese drizzle. Sure, you could opt for one of the four different Benedicts on the breakfast and brunch menu. Or you could choose the s'mores french toast or even the house-made biscuits, but these waffles are the restaurant's signature dish for a very good reason. Moist and luscious, they're more dessert than breakfast. In addition to its fantastic early-morning offerings, Terrace also serves lunch and dinner. Remarkably for a menu that holds such choices as the red velvet waffles, Terrace actually prides itself on its healthy options that have been given a stamp of approval from a YMCA nutritionist. Choices like the Terrace Fruit Salad with its baby greens, fruit, and sliced chicken breast are approved for the health conscious. But those who aren't on a diet will find plenty of dishes to satisfy here as well. Dinner should be started with a bowl of the lump blue crab bisque with a touch of sherry and plenty of cream, and followed with the Terrace Fried

Chicken served alongside garlic mashed potatoes and crumbled pork gravy. Now if only you could talk them into bringing out a few of those red velvet waffles for dessert. See Executive Chef Thomas Kerns' recipe for **Banana Bread French Toast** on p. 243.

Toscana, 6401 Morrison Blvd., SouthPark, Charlotte, NC 28211; (704) 367-1808; conterestaurantgroup.com; Italian; $$$. It would be hard to find a spot more suited to appearing like a European courtyard than this tucked-away restaurant in the specialty shops across from SouthPark Mall. From the patio you can enjoy the nearby fountain—and people watching those perusing the upscale shopping area. Both lunch and dinner are available, featuring authentic Italian offerings. Your best bet is to start with the simple arugula salad featuring organic peppery arugula topped with cherry tomatoes and *grana padano* cheese, and drizzled in a balsamic vinaigrette. A beef carpaccio is so tender that the texture of the meat, topped with white truffle oil, is almost buttery. The menu is as traditionally Italian as it comes, with a selection of decadent pastas and rich entrees. For a well-made and creamy choice, order the carbonara, made with house-made spaghetti, egg, cacao cheese, ground black pepper, *guanciale,* and smoked pancetta. The smoky flavor of the meats only enhances the sweetness of the cream and cheese. Finish your meal in true Italian fashion with freshly made biscotti served alongside a sweet Tuscan dessert wine.

Upstream, 6902 Phillips Place Ct., SouthPark, Charlotte, NC 28210; (704) 556-7730; harpersgroup.com/upstream; Seafood; $$$. The only way you're going to feel closer to the ocean in this landlocked city is if you put a conch shell up to your ear. At this cool, sleek SouthPark restaurant, you'll find fresh dayboat seafood and some of the best sushi in town. You'll also find a bar bites menu and signature cocktails that make this the perfect spot to settle in on one of the soft patio chairs or at the bar for a few snacks and drinks early in the evening. Dishes like the ahi tuna tacos topped with wasabi aioli and pickled ginger or the sweet and sour crispy shrimp are perfect pairings for fresh, sweet drinks like the Cucumber Cooler cocktail with slices of fresh cucumber, Tanqueray, and a hint of fresh lime juice. Brightly flavored cocktails like this also pair well with many of the menu's offerings like the citrusy white shrimp and avocado ceviche or one of the specialty sushi rolls like the Spicy Hawaiian Tuna Roll, featuring peppered tuna, asparagus, and mango. While lunch and dinner are excellent hours to visit this sophisticated spot, one of the best times to stop by is for Sunday brunch when for $24.95 per person you can indulge in a raw bar, fresh-rolled sushi, made-to-order omelets, and plenty of other breakfast and brunch offerings. Paired with a glass of their Prosecco or Champagne, there's no better way to start a relaxing Sunday.

Village Tavern, 4201 Congress St., SouthPark, Charlotte, NC 28209; (704) 552-9983; villagetavern.com; American; $$. For a spot that started in a charming historic village in Winston-Salem, the location of this outpost is lacking its forefather's ambience. But while it may be in the bottom of an office building, this tavern still manages a cozy feel alongside its quality food. The menu offers longtime favorites like a creamy hot crab dip made with tender chunks of crab meat and served with buttery triangles of toasted garlic bread for scooping up the chunky dip. Salads here aren't the dainty kinds you'll find some places, but rather come piled high on your plate with toppings. And while there are always new options among the specialties, classics like the grilled meatloaf made from a family recipe or the oversize Maryland-style crab cakes are worth the order every time. When it comes to ending dinner, the dessert menu offers plenty to satisfy your sweet tooth, including cakes and pies, but some of the best options are dessert drinks like the Ice Cream Toasted Almond with French vanilla ice cream, dark crème de cacao, Amaretto, and vodka.

Vivace, 1100 Metropolitan Ave., Midtown, Charlotte, NC 28204; (704) 370-7755; vivacecharlotte.com; Italian; $$$. With valet parking, a swanky bar scene, and an open kitchen producing chic Italian fare, Vivace was an instant hit among the city's most stylish. The adjacent patio offers skyline views over the nearby greenway and is the perfect sunny spot for an early evening drink or midday lunch. Inside you'll find two levels of dining with an airy open first floor, and a cozier second story, also offering views of the glittering skyline in the evenings. If you're here for lunch, the paninis are a must and if you're looking to indulge, try the short rib version with tender meat pressed between the crusty fresh bread. For dinner start your meal with one of the restaurant's cured meat and cheese plates. The meats are cured in house and options like the Milano salami pair well with a glass of one of the Italian wines. Pizzas are served thin crust from a brick oven and come with gourmet toppings like duck *confit* with currants and balsamic onion or rich and melted four-cheese with tender portobello mushrooms and caramelized onions. If you're in the mood for a simple pasta with plenty of flavor, the *pappardelle alla bolognese* features thick al dente pasta tossed in a meaty sauce with goat-cheese cream. End the evening with dessert like the espresso cheesecake and a cup of cappuccino and consider your trip to Italy via Midtown complete.

Yama Asian Fusion, 720 Governor Morrison St., SouthPark, Charlotte, NC 28211; (704) 295-0905; yamaasianfusion.com; Japanese/Sushi; $$$. This may not be the trendiest sushi spot in town (read: the music isn't blaring and the roll names aren't particularly provocative), but rest assured, the creative rolls you'll find here are some of the best in the city. The boisterous restaurant generally hosts a mix of SouthPark families and young groups in its inviting dining rooms and small outdoor patio. After sitting down you'll be given a warm washcloth to clean your hands before digging into dishes like fresh, firm edamame and a long list of sushi rolls. The wine and sake list is extensive—or, if you prefer to bring your own, Yama allows for guests to bring bottles from The Wine Store next door with no corkage fee. While the menu does include hibachi grilled items and other Asian fusion dishes, sushi is the specialty with tasty rolls like the Rock 'n' Roll, featuring crab, avocado, and cream cheese wrapped in white fish tempura and drizzled in a spicy sauce. Yama also offers one of the more creative desserts in town with their sweet and creamy green tea crème brulée—an unexpectedly delicious fusion of Eastern and Western flavors.

Zebra Restaurant, 4521 Sharon Rd., SouthPark, Charlotte, NC 28211; (704) 442-9525; zebrarestaurant.net; French; $$$. Like many of the wines and cheeses it serves, this upscale French restaurant only seems to get better with age. A nightly tasting menu and a wine list featuring more than 900 bottles are the types of things that make Zebra continue to rise above the competition. And while you'd never expect it from a dinner trip to its elegant dining rooms, Zebra also offers breakfast, which means you can have the opportunity to enjoy Chef and Owner Jim Alexander's skills in the kitchen with lower-priced items like his fluffy, stuffed omelets. But Alexander's culinary talent really shines in the evenings when diners have the opportunity to taste one of the menu's many variations of *foie gras* (try the seared "slider" version with pancetta crisp) or the signature Angel Hair Basket with beef tenderloin, shrimp, lobster, and scallops in a tangle of crisp angel hair pasta. The desserts are worth ordering, but if you happen to skip, don't worry. Zebra includes a small taste of the day's dessert with the check—if you're lucky, that dessert will be a moist sliver of the house-made pistachio cake.

Zink American Kitchen, 4310 Sharon Rd., SouthPark, Charlotte, NC 28211; (704) 909-5500; harpersgroup.com/zink; American; $$$. This restaurant was once located in the heart of Uptown on Tryon St. However, it really seemed to hit its stride when it brought its urban vibe to the center of SouthPark. The menu here is designed to be comfort food with a twist, which means you'll find dishes like a decadent lobster mac and cheese or bacon-wrapped meatloaf. And the atmosphere adds its own twist with the restaurant's signature 30-foot zinc bar, as well as a large patio with expansive views of the SouthPark scene. Whether you're in the mood for one of the wood-oven flatbreads or meats from the wood-fired grill, weekend nights are a great time to stop in when Zink offers live music until late in the evening and drink specials from their extensive wine, beer, and cocktail lists.

Landmarks

Cajun Queen, 1800 E. 7th St., Elizabeth, Charlotte, NC 28204; (704) 377-9017; cajunqueen.com; Cajun; $$. If you're in town during Mardi Gras—or just craving Cajun fare—this is the place to go for a taste of the Big Easy. With live jazz nightly upstairs and a festive atmosphere in its historic Elizabeth setting, the Cajun Queen has been offering the Queen City a glimpse of Nawlins for decades. Appropriately dominated by seafood, the menu features all the favorites: sautéed crawfish tails, shrimp gumbo, étouffée, and blackened catfish. For dessert, the creamy bread pudding is a must-order and should be accompanied by one of the specialty coffees for the full French Quarter-meets-Charlotte experience.

Fenwick's, 511 Providence Rd., Myers Park, Charlotte, NC 28207; (704) 333-2750; fenwicksonprovidence.com; American/Cajun; $$. Stop in at this cozy Myers Park restaurant and you're likely to be among regulars. The folks who come here know the servers, bartenders, and even each other—after all, they've been open and a local favorite since 1984. The owners have ties to Louisiana so you're likely to find a few Cajun specials on the menu, like a slightly spicy gumbo with savory veggies. But for the most part the menu is simple and American with appetizers like fried chicken fingers, sandwiches, and burgers, and casual entrees like a filling chicken and broccoli casserole. And if you enjoyed lunch or dinner, stop in on Sunday when you'll find selections like a crab cake Benedict and homemade coffeecake with strawberry butter. Give it a visit or two and soon you too will start feeling like a regular.

The Original Pancake House, 915 Charlottetowne Ave., Midtown, Charlotte, NC 28204; (704) 372-7099; originalpancake house.com; American/Breakfast; $. The name of this restaurant could actually be The Original Power Breakfast Spot. It might not be quite as enticing for pancake-lovers, but especially on Friday mornings this is the place to see and be seen when it comes to the city's public officials. During the rest of the week, you'll find families, couples, and the occasional businessmen chowing down on hearty breakfasts. There are other options—waffles, omelets, and even crepes, to name a few. This place got its name for a reason. For a twist on the ordinary, try the potato pancakes. Served with sour cream or cinnamon applesauce, they're a sweet departure from the typical buttermilk. Or, for an extra sweet and Southern version of the flapjacks, opt for the Georgia Pecan Pancakes, which are filled and topped with hot toasted pecans and drenched in hot syrup. Seeing and being seen never tasted so good.

Specialty Stores, Markets & Producers

Clean Catch Fish Market, 2820 Selwyn Ave., Myers Park, Charlotte 28209; (704) 333-1212; cleancatchfish.com. Before this small fish market arrived in Myers Park, finding truly fresh fish in the city could be a challenge. But with the arrival of this shop—and its wild salmon, littleneck clams, snapper, grouper, cobia, yellowfin tuna, lump crab meat, swordfish and more—problems finding fish fresh from the sea are a thing of the past. But this isn't your old-fashioned fish monger. At Clean Catch they utilize modern technology from bringing in fish from around the world to using their Twitter handle (@CleanCatchFish) to broadcast what's in the shop that day. Think something sounds tasty? Text them your name, fish, quantity, and any other specifics and your fish will be waiting when you pick it up. Just make sure you check early in the day as these fish are swooped up fast.

Dean & Deluca, 6903 Phillips Place Ct., SouthPark, Charlotte, NC 28210; (704) 643-6868; deandeluca.com. The city's most stylish always seem to be mingling in the dining area and on the patio of this chic New York import. With aisles of gourmet foods and cases filled with high-end, pre-made dishes, it's no wonder SouthPark's most sophisticated have deemed this one of their favorite places to shop and dine. At lunchtime the shop is especially full with locals grabbing freshly made sushi, salads, soups, and sandwiches before pulling up a seat at one of the indoor cafe tables or under an umbrella on the outdoor side-walk. A coffee station and entire case of chocolate delicacies round out the experi-ence—and are likely to tempt you back up to the counter long after you've finished that healthy salad.

Earth Fare, 721 Governor Morrison St., SouthPark, Charlotte, NC 28211; (704) 749-5042; earthfare.com. Want a hard-to-find beer? Looking for a rare cheese? Need to pick up some fresh, local vege-tables? Hoping to stock up on your grains and granola? Want a freshly prepared meal with absolutely no work attached? Looking for one of the city's best salad bars? Searching for organic beauty products and vitamins? Hoping to find international products from places like Asia and Latin America? Seeking a carefully crafted wine selection with a variety of price points? If you happened to answer yes to any of these questions, then this upscale SouthPark market should be your next stop.

King's Drive Farmers' Market, 938 S. Kings Dr., Midtown, Charlotte, NC 28204; (704) 332-6366. By far the city's most popular farmers' market, this busy corner of town is a frenetic center of activity on Saturday morning in the summer. The market (April to October) includes a plant section in the summer, pumpkins in the fall, and Christmas trees during the holiday season. Open Tuesday, Friday, and Saturday, it offers local veggies, meats, breads, eggs, jarred goods, fruits, and flowers. For the top picks go early in the day, but half the fun of this experience is catching the crowds who pile in post-breakfast to pick up the city's freshest produce.

New York Butcher Shoppe, 2904 Selwyn Ave., Myers Park, Charlotte, NC 28209; (980) 207-1810; nybutcher.net. Whether you're a rookie in the kitchen or a pro behind the grill, this Myers Park shop has a fresh cut of meat for you. Peruse an impressive selection of pork, beef, and chicken as well as more unexpected meats like elk and rabbit. Your best option here is to ask the guys behind the counter. Not only will they direct you on what to order, but they'll also tell you how to prepare it and often point you in the direction of a tasty marinade or rub. While the shop is small, you'll also find a sandwich section, pre-made dishes, wines, and a variety of appetizer options—all perfect for tossing in your bag to enjoy alongside your slice of meat.

Pasta & Provisions, 1528 Providence Rd., Myers Park, Charlotte, NC 28207; (704) 364-2622; pastaprovisions.com. This family-owned Italian grocer makes its own pasta in house, which means that while the Boar's Head meats, homemade soups, and wine offerings may look tempting, don't even think about leaving without at least one of the fresh pastas. Noodles can be purchased by the pound and in addition to the long ones, the charming Myers Park spot also offers raviolis in flavors like a seasonal sweet potato or a decadent lobster and crab version. And if you happen to be there on a day when they're selling the house-made gnocchi, a pillowy dumpling created with ricotta cheese, make sure to add that to your basket. Your dinner guests will thank you later.

petit philippe, 2820 Selwyn Ave., Myers Park, Charlotte, NC 28209; (704) 332-9910; petitphilippe.com. This is a shop dedicated entirely to fine wine and gourmet chocolate, proving at the very least that fantasies can be a reality. Locally owned and operated, the shop offers wines from California, the Pacific Northwest, and Europe. The impressive wine selection is curated by Co-owner and Sommelier

Mark Hickey, while the chocolate is created in house by his Le Cordon Bleu–trained Pastry Chef and wife, Casey. The chic, contemporary interior is the perfect place to meet for a glass of wine and a plate of chocolates. Or, if you're looking for something to wrap up and take home, order chocolates ahead of time in unique flavors like strawberry balsamic, crème brulée, and *fleur de sel*. Beautifully wrapped and paired with a bottle of wine, this may be the best hostess gift in town.

South Charlotte

Ballantyne, Blakeney, Pineville, Matthews & Stonecrest

Charlotte's southern realms are the newest additions to the growing city. Only a few years ago, much of this region south of I-485 was covered in farmland and the occasional country store. Nowadays the area features big and bright new shopping centers scattered among attractive housing developments.

South of the city you'll also find several small, charming town centers such as Matthews or Waxhaw, where historical buildings set the scene and life seems to move at a slightly slower pace. These are the kind of places where you'll want to spend a Saturday meandering through a local farmers' market, checking out the side-street antiques shops, and indulging in small-town restaurants where locals wave to each other on their way to their tables.

Places like Ballantyne, Stonecrest, and the Arboretum offer a bustling and bold alternative to these small towns. Brimming with new shops with national names, popular movie theaters, and busy restaurants and bars, these shopping centers offer plenty of year-round enjoyment, from summer concert series to winter holiday celebrations.

With its varied communities and residents, South Charlotte is full of culinary surprises. Among these restaurants you'll find elegant, locally sourced food served in a former brothel and a spot serving some of the city's most upscale tapas tucked into a shopping mall. Don't let appearances deceive—this part of town offers plenty of places for delicious dining and a taste of local culture.

Foodie Faves

Akropolis Kafe, 14027 Conlan Circle, Ballantyne, Charlotte, NC 28277; (704) 714-1113; akropoliskafe.com; Greek/Mediterranean; $. Simple and straightforward, this small cafe has been serving Mediterranean fare since 1978. While most of the menu is traditional Greek foods like gyros, souvlaki, spanakopita, and mousaka, there are plenty of Mediterranean and Persian offerings as well. Hummus and falafel platters are great starters and hearty rice entrees include a chicken kabob on rice and a marinated pork tenderloin on rice. Some of the best options are the sandwiches, like the super gyro with sautéed onions, green peppers, and tomato, or the veggie sandwich, featuring warm pita bread stuffed with lettuce, tomato, onion, cucumber, feta, and plenty of creamy tzatziki sauce. Served with hot, thick-cut fries or a fresh Greek salad, the sandwiches, and the rest of the menu, are available for take-out—an option many frequent customers choose. And if your little one isn't the type to dig into adventurous dishes like lamb or falafel, don't despair. The children's menu here offers your typical kid's fare with a Greek twist (think pita pizza). And, of course, the flaky, sweet baklava for dessert is the perfect finish to your Mediterranean meal.

Bad Daddy's Burger Bar, 15105A John J. Delaney Dr., Ballantyne, Charlotte, NC 28277; (704) 919-2700; baddaddys burgerbar.com; Hamburgers; $. The original Dilworth version of this restaurant draws its fair share of the family crowd, but this South Charlotte outpost is kid-central many nights. Of course this makes complete sense considering this is a spot selling some of the best burgers and fries in town alongside creamy milk shakes and crispy fried pickles. But grown-ups need not worry. After all, there's plenty on the menu just for you. While the little ones slurp up their PB & J shakes, you can indulge in the spiked cookies-and-cream version made with vodka, Kahlùa, Bailey's, and Oreo cookies, or try the Grass Hopper, made with rum, crème de menthe green, and crème de cocoa white. More in the mood for a burger and beer? Sip on the Harpoon IPA, which Bad Daddy's recommends alongside the Mama Ricotta's Burger. And that's a very grown-up burger, too—topped with house-made mozzarella, pesto, vine-ripened tomatoes, pepperoncinis, and extra-virgin olive oil, this is Italy on a bun. Or, for an even more unusual twist, try the Sam Adams Boston Lager along-side the Sam I Am burger, made with American

GREAT SCOT!

Step inside the Ballantyne's intimate **Gallery Bar** and you'll feel you've been transported to an elegant lodge complete with dark wood accents, dim lamp lighting, and a long marble bar. But it's what is behind the bar that makes this spot really special.

 Here you'll find one of the city's best selections of fine scotches—there are more than 50 carefully selected choices (you can view the list on their website). Interested in imbibing? The bar offers scotch flights and even hosts monthly meetings of a Scotch Society of Ballantyne, pairing the spirit with food and learning. The meetings are $35 per person and are open to hotel guests as well as the public. But make your reservations ahead of time because space is limited and the meetings fill up fast with those in search of a taste of the Highlands. 10000 Ballantyne Commons Pkwy., 28277; (704) 248-4100; gallery-restaurant.com.

cheese, over-easy fried egg, rosemary ham, and fresh pesto. Looks like those kids will have to get in line.

Bangkok Ocha, 7629 Pineville Matthews Rd., Charlotte, NC 28226; (704) 544-7770; Thai; $$. Don't even think about dismissing this tasty Thai spot just because of its pedestrian location in a South Charlotte strip mall. While the interior leaves a little to be desired (low ceilings and bright green carpet don't make for the most stylish eating experience), the menu full of authentic Thai fare won't leave you wanting. For a taste, stop in for lunch when their $7.95 special includes a drink, soup, spring roll, rice, and a main. But to really dig in to the dishes, come at dinner when the family-run kitchen is serving up a delicate pad thai, rich curries, and a tasty chicken-basil stir fry. The best time of all to come may be on Wednesday, which is the only day they offer their savory hot-and-sour soup—something worth the trip all on its own.

Beantown Tavern, 130 Matthews Station St., Matthews, NC 28105; (704) 849-2023; beantowntavern.com; Pub; $$. If you're ever looking for a place to catch a Red Sox game in Charlotte—or just a taste of New England—this is your place. Owned by a former Boston resident and longtime Sox fan, Beantown Tavern features traditional Boston fare, drinks, and sports. Order up a cold Samuel Adams and a Boston Fish Filet sandwich made with Cajun remoulade and served on a fresh hoagie roll. Or, try the Boston Cheesesteak made with onions and peppers and topped with melted white American cheese. The menu is large and varied, though, with options ranging from pizzas, calzones, and pastas, to seafood and ribs. And, of course, the Boston Cream Pie is a must for dessert. But while the food here is decent pub grub, the entertainment and nightly drink specials are what draw in the fans. When it's not game night for the Sox, Patriots, or even a Boston college team, you'll find karaoke and occasionally live music. Stop in for a drink and to feel transported about 800 miles north. Just don't even think about wearing your Yankees cap.

Big View Diner, 16637 Lancaster Hwy., Charlotte, NC 28277; (704) 544-0313; bigviewdiner.com; Diner/Greek/Hamburgers; $. Step inside this large retro diner and your eye is immediately drawn to the glass cases near the door. Brimming with pies, tarts, cookies, and pastries, these cases with their oversize desserts set the tone for the kind of big eating you'll be doing at Big View. Located south of Ballantyne, the diner's interior is a stunning mix of deep reds and golds, tiled floors, and plenty of tables—both inside and on the exterior patio. You can expect to wait on weekends when families crowd in for the popular brunch and breakfast fare. But lunch and dinner offer plenty of their own exciting options like the classic chicken and waffles made with crispy chicken tenders, Belgian waffles, and a warm pecan buttered syrup, or the barbecue pork ribs, slow smoked and topped with a house-made barbecue sauce. The Greek owners incorporate much of their own heritage into dishes like the Spinach Pie with spinach, leeks, fresh dill, and feta cheese baked into a delicate phyllo. And forget about the diet entirely here because the fresh house-made desserts deserve your undivided attention. And in true diner fashion, there's even a dish with a competitive edge. If you can finish it by yourself, The Triple "D" dessert is free. Of course, this means eating chocolate cake, one scoop of each ice cream, whipped cream, chocolate, caramel, nuts, bananas, and cherries. Think you're up for the challenge?

Blackthorne Restaurant & Bar, 11318 N. Community House Rd., Ballantyne, Charlotte, NC 28277; (704) 817-5554; blackthornerestaurant.com; American/French; $$$. Tucked in Ballantyne Corners Shopping Center, one of this bistro's best offerings may be its rooftop patio. The casual bar and seating area offers great views and occasional live music. The Executive Chef, Mark Hibbs, has long been a favorite on the city's restaurant scene for his creative menus featuring innovative, local fare. There is a large selection of small plates, all perfect for sharing over wine on either the patio or the cozy dining area. Try the seared duck breast crostini, featuring tender slices of the duck topped with caramelized onions and cranberry compote. Or for a casual twist on a gourmet meat, order the fried quail bucket with eight pieces of chicken-fried quail served alongside buttermilk biscuits and rosemary gravy. Dishes like the braised lamb shank and roasted half chicken may look familiar from other menus Hibbs has manned. But creative dishes like a venison meatloaf made with onions, garlic, and blueberries are the kind of thing that really shows off this chef's talent. And speaking of creativity Blackthorne's bartenders show off their skills with drinks like a Bacon Manhattan, which features bourbon, smoked maple syrup, and candied bacon, practically making it a meal on its own.

The Blue Taj, 14815 Ballantyne Village Way, Ballantyne, Charlotte, NC 28277; (704) 369-5777; thebluetaj.com; Indian; $$$. Owned by the folks behind **Copper** (p. 56) in Dilworth, this elegant and intimate Indian restaurant is often a surprise find for those in the area. Located next to the entrance of a movie theater, the inside's sophisticated and modern ambience features walls painted with abstract shapes and images, and orange accents enhancing the dimly lit dining area. Indian fare fans will be pleased to find favorites on this menu like a classic saag paneer made with spinach and fresh cheese or the makahani chicken served in a creamy tomato sauce with a slight honey flavor. Seafood options are also delicious and elegantly plated, such as the Kolmino Patio, made with tender jumbo shrimp sautéed with spices and a tamarind glaze or the Scallop Nilgiri Kurma, featuring scallops flavored with a cashew curry sauce. Whatever you do start your meal with the airy, fragrant naan and end it with the dense and sweet Malai Kulfi, a housemade Indian ice cream flavored with saffron and rose water.

Brixx Wood-Fired Pizza, 9820 Rea Rd., Blakeney, Charlotte, NC 28277; (704) 940-2011; brixxpizza.com; Italian; $$. The restaurant's interior is always a lively mix of families and friends, but it's the patio overlooking the fountains and playground where you'll typically find the crowds at this Blakeney spot. In addition to all your usual favorites (think Margherita, Hawaiian, and *quatro formaggio*) the Brixx also offers plenty of unique signature pizzas worth trying. Dig into options such as the pear and Gorgonzola topped with caramelized onions and toasted walnuts or the Pimento Cheese Pizza made with jalapeño pimento cheese, roasted red peppers, crumbled bacon, and spinach leaves. Plus the restaurant makes it easy for everyone to enjoy a slice with vegan and even gluten-free options. And while pizza is the star here, there are plenty of other choices like sandwiches made using the fresh-baked focaccia bread or salads featuring locally grown vegetables. Whatever you choose enjoy it alongside one of their local craft brews or a playful cocktail like the Pizza-tini—chilled Grey Goose and dry vermouth with two olives stuffed with spicy pepperoni.

Buca di Beppo, 10915 Carolina Place Pkwy., Pineville, NC 28134; (704) 542-5146; bucadibeppo.com; Italian; $$. This Italian restaurant may be a chain, but its hearty dishes served family-style and friendly servers give the place a neighborhood feel. You'll likely be dining to the crooning of Dean Martin or Frank Sinatra and walls covered by photos of Italian-American icons give Buca a cozy vibe. The options here are inspired by Northern and Southern Italy and you'll find plenty of the pastas and pizzas any Italian food lover craves. Start with the chopped antipasto salad made with diced pepperoni, red onions, pepperoncinis, cucumbers, tomatoes, provolone, feta, and Gorgonzola and then tossed in an Italian vinaigrette. Then, if you're feeling hungry, order a few of the decadent pastas for the table. The Bucatini Ala Enzo comes with pancetta and fried prosciutto with sautéed mushrooms and peas, while the slightly spicy Shrimp Fra Diavolo comes with sautéed garlic shrimp in a rosa sauce and penne pasta. With a full menu of heaping portions of meats, pizzas, pastas, seafood, and sides, it's nearly impossible to have any room left for dessert. But if you do, order the tiramisu made with homemade ladyfingers soaked in dark rum and espresso. You'll almost be sorry you have to share.

Cajun Yard Dog, 8036 Providence Rd., Arboretum, Charlotte, NC 28277; (704) 752-1750; cajunyarddog.net; Cajun; $$. Couldn't make it to Mardi Gras this year? Don't worry, this casual restaurant complete with Mardi Gras T-shirts on the walls and beads strung around the bar is serving up authentic Cajun staples that will cure your cravings for French Quarter fare. Tucked away in the Arboretum Shopping Center, this small spot is serving up crawfish etouffee, red beans and rice, po' boys, crab cakes, and fried chicken, all alongside an offering of 35 different varieties of hot sauce. And while the entrees include sure-to-please options like shrimp and andouille pasta or a hearty seafood jambalaya, the hard-to-find Cajun-style meatloaf may be the menu's top choice. Made with a mix of beef and pork and topped with a rich tomato gravy, this is home-style Cajun cooking at its best. Order it alongside the fried okra and squash casserole for the full Southern experience. Then finish the meal with slice of pecan pie and consider your Louisiana excursion complete.

Cantina 1511, 7708 Rea Rd., Stonecrest, Charlotte, NC 28277; (704) 752-9797; cantina1511restaurant.com; Mexican; $$. Like its Dilworth predecessor, this Mexican restaurant is a favorite for those in search of authentic Mexican fare—as well as those who just want their traditional chips and salsa, tableside guacamole, and a tasty taco or two. This version next to Stonecrest shopping center is a little larger, but still offers the same south-of-the-border ambience and lively bar area. The best seats in the house may be in the semiprivate booths where there's plenty of room on the table for piling on your favorite spicy foods. Start with a margarita and orders of the guacamole made tableside and the Cantina 1511 Fundido made with Mexican cheese, fresh herbs, jala-peño bacon, roasted pineapples, and onions, all served with flour tortillas. If the appetizers alone don't fill you up, dig into options like enchiladas, tacos, and carnitas. And while the menu offers plenty of exotic options inspired by the owner's trips to Mexico City, some of the tastiest choices are unexpectedly the quesadillas. Take, for instance, a quesadilla made with avocado, lump crab, jalapeño bacon, and mixed Mexican cheeses or one made with tender slivers of carne asada steak, caramelized poblano peppers and onions, and creamy Mexican cheeses. Still not full? Finish the meal up with the restaurant's famed tres leches cake.

Cosmos Cafe, 8420 Rea Rd., Charlotte, NC 28277; (704) 544-5268; cosmoscafe.com; American/Sushi; $$. While there's no doubt that the Uptown location of this bar and restaurant is popular, the South Charlotte version may have actually surpassed it when it comes to the nightlife scene. This might seem surprising as the Rea Rd. version is smack in the middle of suburbia, but perhaps its location outside of Uptown's bustle is exactly what draws in the crowds on weekend evenings. While Cosmos is a family-friendly restaurant by day, in the evenings top DJs, stylish crowds, and one of the city's best bartenders make this a hot nightlife spot. If it's food you're searching for, though, come on a sunny afternoon when the patio is open and start with some of the cafe's tasty tapas. From 5 p.m. to 7 p.m. each day, patrons can get two for one tapas, which means more opportunities to enjoy dishes like the hot and creamy roasted artichoke dip or the braised beef empanadas filled with tender meat and served over smoked chili salsa. In the mood for something with more of an Asian twist? Try the sushi. The selection is large and includes creative rolls like the sweet and spicy Cherry Bloom Roll made with tuna, tempura shrimp, and avocado topped with wasabi, eel sauce, and a spicy sauce. One of the most popular times to stop by Cosmos—especially with the kids—is for the $12 Sunday brunch buffet featuring all your favorites (think french toast, bacon, grits, muffins, eggs, and home fries) as well as freshly made pancakes.

D'Vine Wine Cafe, 14815 Ballantyne Village Way, Ballantyne, Charlotte, NC 28277; (704) 369-5050; dvinewinecafe.com; French/Tapas; $. This cafe, which opens into a retail wine shop, offers gourmet fare and a laid-back vibe. While wine reigns here, there are also more than 20 specialty beers offered in this cozy spot. Plus, in addition to drinks and food, you'll find live music most nights and a relaxing patio. Dishes are designed to pair well with one of the more than 35 wines by the glass and you'll want to try options like the apple and fig toasted focaccia drizzled in a brie sauce or the pork medallions served with bacon mac and cheese and a tangy barbecue sauce. Most of the menu features small plates designed for sharing, as well as cheese and charcuterie options. However, there are a few larger plates worth trying, like the *filet au poivre* served with roasted potatoes, mushrooms, and asparagus, or the shrimp and grits made with shrimp, pork belly, and stone-ground grits with a sherry sauce. Knowledgeable servers are great to guiding you to the perfect glass or bottle to enjoy alongside your choice. And while the dessert menu is small (there are only two options most nights), it more than makes up for it in flavor. This is an ideal place to stop in later in the evening to split a bottle on the patio and dig into an innovative sweet option like the poached pear–bacon crisp with maple mousse. Cheers!

18 Asian & Sushi Bar, 9935 Rea Rd., Blakeney, Charlotte, NC 28277; (704) 845-1801; 18blakeney.com; Sushi; $$. Owned by the

Chens, a family who owns several other Asian fusion restaurants around the city, this is the perfect spot for those craving sushi south of I-485. The crowd here most nights is a comfortable mix of families enjoying rice or noodle bowls alongside couples and convivial groups. The U-shaped bar is typically full on weekend evenings with locals taking advantage of cocktails and sake. Serious fans of sushi can dig into the deluxe sample platter ($24.95), which includes California rolls alongside a large selection of nigiri. And if you prefer your sushi to be of the cooked variety or to have an unexpected twist, you've come to the right place. Take, for instance, the Hawaiian Sunset roll, a tempura shrimp, avocado, and spicy tuna roll topped in red tobiko and a sweet peach sauce or the Tokyo Triangle, made with deep-fried rice wrapped inside out with avocado, cream cheese, tuna, and salmon and then topped with spicy mayo and red tobiko. These are decadent rolls, and while the fish is tasty and fresh, it's often barely the focus of the flavor here.

Firebirds Wood Fired Grill, 7716 Rea Rd., Charlotte, NC 28277; (704) 752-7979; firebirdsrestaurants.com; American/Seafood/ Steakhouse; $$. There have been Firebirds in the Charlotte area since 2000 and while the chain is based on the idea of flavors from Colorado, it has been happily adopted by Carolinians. The first thing you'll notice in the restaurant is its smoky fragrance from its cozy indoor stone fireplace and hardwood flames used in the kitchen. The next thing you'll notice are the hearty portion sizes of dishes like pecan-crusted trout, baby back ribs, and meatloaf served alongside mashed potatoes and green beans. The bar here—as at all local Firebirds locations—fills up on the weekends with 20- and 30-somethings indulging in creative cocktails like the Cucumber Gimlet, a mix of Hendrick's Gin with fresh-squeezed lime juice, cilantro, and cucumber. Stop in for a drink between 3 p.m. and 7 p.m. on any weeknight and you can enjoy half-priced appetizers like lobster spinach *queso* or seared ahi tuna alongside it.

The Flying Biscuit Café, 7930 Rea Rd., Stonecrest, Charlotte, NC 28277; (704) 295-4440; flyingbiscuit.com; American/Breakfast/ Southern; $$. See description on p. 62.

Gallery Restaurant, 10000 Ballantyne Commons Pkwy., Ballantyne, Charlotte, NC 28277; (704) 248-4100; gallery-restaurant.com; American; $$$. Located in the bottom of the prestigious Ballantyne Hotel, this elegant restaurant offers con- temporary, farm-to-fork dishes for breakfast, lunch, and dinner. While breakfast and lunch offer plenty of tasty options—and convenience for those staying in the hotel—the dinner menu is the star. The dining room fea- tures yellow accents, white tablecloths, and candle lighting, while friendly, fast servers bring out sophisticated dishes at a perfect pace. Known for its impressive scotch selection, it's a good idea to start with a cocktail before choosing from the impressive wine list.

If you're in the mood for a real culinary adventure, Gallery offers a chef's tasting menu including either five courses for $65 or seven courses for $80. The chef is dedicated to incorporating meats and veggies from local farms and you'll find the season's freshest produce in many of the dishes. Opting out of the tasting menu? Begin with the caramelized Vidalia onion soup made with sweet onions and topped with focaccia crostini and Guinness-soaked gruyère cheese. While the entrees are fairly straightforward with offerings like smoked duck breast, a filet mignon, and a salmon with ricotta dumplings, each is full of flavor. For an especially decadent—and delicious—dish, indulge in the braised short rib of beef served with local grits and crispy goat cheese, and topped with house-made peach and blueberry barbecue sauce. Like what you ordered? Gallery offers cooking schools with hands-on opportunities for creating—and eating—the chef's best. See Chef de Cuisine J. Kelly Morrow's recipe for **French Onion Soup** on p. 247.

Harry's Grille and Tavern, 2127 Ayrsley Town Blvd., Charlotte, NC 29273; (704) 499-9494; harrysgrilleandtavern.com; American; $$. Plan on bringing a designated driver when you visit this bright and cheerful Ayrsley restaurant—or at least staying for awhile. The cocktails here are so good that stopping at just one is never easy—trying to decide between the famed Whiskey Sour and the Champagne with elderflower is just too difficult. Luckily there are plenty of small plates to enjoy alongside your cocktails, like the chilled sesame noodles served in a peanut sauce that comes with a slightly spicy kick or the five-spice-crusted pork tenderloin alongside house-made spiced mango chutney. Main courses include a well-curated selection of burgers and sandwiches such as a crab-cake sandwich with Asian pear slaw and wasabi dijon aioli. And, of course, there are the more elegant entrees like the maple-brined pork tenderloin with grilled vegetable ratatouille and the seared salmon encrusted with panko and dijon.

Jim 'n' Nick's Bar-B-Q, 13840 Steele Creek Rd., Charlotte, NC 28278; (704) 930-2290; jimnnicks.com; Barbecue; $$. This barbecue chain is a favorite across the Southeast and Charlotte is no exception. From the minute you settle into your seats in the casual, smoky-scented dining room and are promptly served a basket of steaming hot cheese biscuits, you know you're in a place where good food—and plenty of it—holds a premium. Start with a sweet tea (this is a barbecue restaurant, after all) and an order of the hand-breaded onion rings served golden brown and hot. Then dig into heaping plates like the baby back ribs covered in their signature rub and slow smoked or the pork hot link plate created with seven seasonings and three types of peppers. Of course if you're really going to do their barbecue right, order the Pulled Pork Plate, featuring a classic pork shoulder that's been hand pulled. Enjoy it alongside their creamy, house-made coleslaw or delectable mac and cheese. Unexpectedly one of the best things at Jim 'n' Nicks is the restaurant's taco offering. It only makes the menu on Tuesday, but occasionally, if you ask, they might prepare them on another day. Options include the Bar-B-Q Pork Taco, made with their famed pulled pork and made-from-scratch slaw; the Beef Brisket Taco, stuffed with the slow-smoked meat and topped with pico de gallo; and the Fried Catfish Taco, topped with creamy coleslaw and house-made tartar sauce. They're all wrapped in warm flour tortillas, and they're all mouthwateringly good.

Jojo China Bistro, 7800 Rea Rd., Charlotte, NC 28277; (704) 541-6488; jojo2go; Chinese; $$. Sure, they deliver. And yes, you can even take advantage of curbside pick-up, but the best way to enjoy these large helpings of authentic Chinese food is in the upscale restaurant's modern interior. Find a seat in one of the colorful booths or pull up a stool to the small bar and dig into hard-to-find dishes like a salt-and-pepper soft-shell crab, a pan-fried whole fish, or twice-cooked pork. Of course there are plenty of your usual favorites here as well, including a spicy Szechuan chicken stir-fried with broccoli, bell peppers, and mushrooms, or the Mongolian beef, sliced and served in a hoisin brown sauce. If you're looking for a fun presentation, try the pineapple fried rice with chicken served in a half pineapple, or for a totally different dish, try the shrimp with spinach fried rice—as in, bright green fried rice. Still not sure you prefer eating in over taking out? Go on a Monday or Tuesday night when more than 50 beers are offered for half price.

Le Peep, 8140 Providence Rd., Arboretum, Charlotte, NC 28277; (704) 540-0470; lepeep.com; Breakfast; $. This may be a chain, but those in South Charlotte have adopted Le Peep's enticing breakfasts as their own. Tucked into the Arboretum Shopping Center, the restaurant offers breakfast, brunch, and lunch, but is known for its breakfast fare and friendly servers. Meals should definitely be started with one of the rich coffee drinks like the caramel macchiato, made with creamy caramel, espresso, steamed milk, and a generous drizzle of caramel. Some of the best items on the menu are under the Benedicts, including the Crabby Patty Benedict, featuring two meaty crab cakes topped with perfectly poached eggs and drenched in a savory hollandaise sauce. And while Le Peep's menu is very grown up, from crepes to omelets, many weekend mornings you'll find plenty of families with kids digging into dishes like stuffed french toast or a Belgian waffle.

Libretto's Pizzeria & Italian Kitchen, 15205-A John J. Delaney Dr., Ballantyne, Charlotte, NC 28277; (704) 714-1442; librettos pizzeria.com; Italian; $$. With an original location in Manhattan and a flavorful Italian sauce that reflects it, this pizzeria, which also has a location in Uptown's Epicentre complex, has become a favorite in South Charlotte. The casual Ballantyne spot feature faux brick walls and Tuscan-style accents. An outdoor patio offers a few tables (and occasionally live music) and a casual bar includes several televisions for watching while you eat the cheesy, oversize slices. While there are options other than pizza on the menu, including pastas and calzones, the thin-crust pizza holds the well-deserved focus in this restaurant. There are plenty of create-your-own options with fairly typical toppings, but the specialty pizzas are where you'll find the best choices. Try the veggie-packed Harvest Pizza, made with spinach, broccoli, mushrooms, roasted peppers, olives, and tomatoes, or the San Genarro, topped with Italian sausage, roasted peppers, onions, and fresh mozzarella. If you're in the mood to enjoy your pizza in the privacy of your own home, you're in luck. Libretto's offers delivery and between the Uptown location and South Charlotte, much of the city is covered for those in search of fresh, cheesy pies brought to their doorstep.

The Lodge: A Sportsman's Grill, 7725 Colony Rd., Charlotte, NC 28226; (704) 544-5226; facebook.com/The-Lodge-A-Sportsmans-Grill; American; $$. You'll want to be hungry when you arrive at this casual, family-friendly sports bar. And then you'll want to order the hot fried pickles to at least momentarily satiate that hunger while you take in the eclectic sports decor and enjoy the laid-back atmosphere. The menu's top offerings are the types of things that are a dieter's worst nightmare: a creamy mac and cheese, Kobe beef sliders, crispy garlic tater tots, piled-high cheeseburgers, and a stuffed Philly cheesesteak. A quality beer list and decent wine selection round out the experience. Owned by J. D. Duncan—the guy who concocted the menus at local favorites like **Mac's Speed Shop** (p. 203)—it's no surprise that this is the kind of place where you'll be planning your next visit before you've finished your first.

Mac's Speed Shop, 2414 Sandy Porter Rd., Steele Creek, Charlotte, NC 28273; (704) 504-8500; macsspeedshop.com; Barbecue/Southern; $. This outpost of the South End Mac's is a natural fit for the South Charlotte area. Featuring a family-friendly atmosphere, loads of barbecue, and creative beer selections, it's no wonder this spot fills up from lunchtime until late in the evening. With beer specials and the occasional live music, Mac's draws a casual crowd in search of a laid-back vibe most nights. Of course, most of the crowd is here for the Southern fare, including fried pickles, pimento cheese, grits, stewed okra, and ribs. And nothing on the menu is as beloved as the hand-pulled pork barbecue sandwich served with fresh slaw on a soft bun. Don't even think about ordering the Lil'  Pig version. You're going to want the Mac Daddy and one of their more than 100 beers to wash it down.

Maestro's Bar and Bistro, 207 Johnston Dr., Pineville, NC 28134; (704) 889-2110; maestrosbarandbistro.com; American/French; $$$. If you've made the drive into Pineville, south of Carolina Place Mall, and you're searching for gourmet fare, it's safe to say you're looking for this cozy bistro. In a home that is more than a century old, just off the main street in downtown Pineville, this elegant restaurant, owned by a husband and wife pair, offers dishes like a rosemary-encrusted rack of lamb served in a red wine demi-glace, apple cider and bourbon-glazed salmon alongside a stone-ground grit cake, and pan-sautéed North Atlantic cod severed over a crab and boursin cheese fondue. And while the entrees are just as savory as they sound, the appetizers and desserts tend to steal the show in this historically housed restaurant. A brown sugar and pecan baked brie features a delicately wrapped version of the creamy cheese topped with sweet brown sugar, and maple dijon-glazed shrimp skewers come in a slightly sweet peach and rum glaze. Desserts vary daily, but staples like a delicate crème brulée or a rich chocolate mousse cake are the perfect way to end your meal.

Mellow Mushroom Pizza Bakers, 14835 Ballantyne Village Way, Ballantyne, Charlotte, NC 28277; (704) 369-5300; mellow mushroom.com; Italian; $$. See description on p. 157.

Miro Spanish Grille, 7804 Rea Rd., Stonecrest, Charlotte, NC 28277; (704) 540-7374; mirospanishgrille.com; Spanish/Tapas; $$. Located in Stonecrest shopping center, this simply decorated restaurant is deceptive considering its tapas dishes are full of complex flavors and unexpected combinations. The tapas menu features more than 20 different options and choosing among them is no easy task. Mushrooms sautéed with garlic and wine, Parmesan baked scallops, crispy fried plantains, fried potatoes with a spicy aioli, stuffed chicken croquettes, and grilled pork kabobs in a chimichurri sauce are just a few of the options here, designed for pairing with one of the European wines. There are large dishes as

Spotlight on Waxhaw

A little more than 20 miles south of the city center is Waxhaw, a charming tiny town surrounded by rolling hills, horse farms, and lush woods. The town of less than 3,000 people offers a historic main street where you'll find small shops and a few restaurants, perfect for soaking up the small-town atmosphere.

For a casual afternoon in Waxhaw, stop into **The Dairy Barn** (107 S. Main St., Waxhaw, NC 28173; 704-843-2276). The barn-themed restaurant includes rocking chairs and a small kids "corral" section. Here you'll find casual fare like hot dogs and barbecue sandwiches, but the best reason to stop in is the soft-serve ice cream cones that can be dipped into hard shells like chocolate or cherry.

Just next door in a 100-year-old building, you'll find a more upscale experience at **Rippington's** (109 W. South Main St., Waxhaw, NC 28173; 704-843-4806; rippingtonswaxhaw.com). This bright and cheery restaurant offers lunch and dinner every day as well as brunch on Sundays. Elegant dishes like a pan-seared filet, crab cakes, or Parmesan-encrusted tilapia are menu favorites in this cozy restaurant with views of Main Street.

Waxhaw's top culinary experience may be its seasonal **Farmers' Market** (waxhawfarmersmarket.com). Open Saturday morning from spring into the fall, the charming market plays hosts to many local vendors. The market offers baskets of fresh-grown vegetables and herbs, rows of fresh eggs, bundles of flowers, and the chance to purchase items like baked bread, homemade jam, and pickled products. The best time of year to come may be midsummer, when fresh and fuzzy peaches from nearby farms cover many of the tables. Buy a few because chances are you'll be tempted to bite into one of these sweet treats before you've even left this sunny corner.

well, including *paella Valenciana,* pork tenderloin served with black beans and plantains, and several seafood options, including harder-to-find choices like sea bass and swordfish. If you have the chance, go on a Tuesday night when you'll find live Spanish music, perfect for setting the scene for plenty of tapas tasting. And if you happen to be stopping by on a warm evening, enhance your Mediterranean-style experience with fresh, icy sangria on the attractive patio.

131 Main Restaurant, 9886 Rea Rd., Stonecrest, Charlotte, NC 28277; (704) 544-0131; 131-main.com; American; $$. See description on p. 72.

Passion8 Bistro, 3415 Highway 51, Fort Mill, SC, 29715; (803) 802-7455; passion8bistro.com; American/Italian; $$$. This small, warm bistro located just over the South Carolina line may be the area's best-kept secret. Just off I-77 near Carowinds amusement park, the restaurant is in a former video poker parlor and brothel, and its closest culinary companion is a Bojangles. But step inside and you'll find an elegant dining room with white-tableclothed tables, a cream-colored tapestry ceiling, maroon accent hues, and a low chandelier casting a glow over the entire space. An artisanal cocktail menu and selective wine list offers a nice start to a night here. The menu features dishes that are predominantly Italian, but many offer hints of Asia and France. Meet the couple who owns it and this makes sense. Chef and Owner Luca Annuziata is from Italy, but has spent time cooking around the globe. The farm-to-fork menu changes nightly depending on what Luca has obtained from the farmers that day, but there are a few popular standouts that show up often, such as veal chops served in plum sauce alongside savory collard greens or pork belly with a rutabaga and cinnamon puree and onion curry *coulis*. And the one dish they never take off the menu is the lightly fried calamari. Served with sweet jalapeño butter, the appetizer is a favorite many customers come searching for. Thinking of skipping dessert? Don't. Dishes like a spice rum *baba* with a saffron Chantilly cream or the pumpkin bread pudding are too good to pass up.

Pure Taqueria, 111 Matthews Station St., Matthews, NC 28105; (704) 841-7873; puretaqueria.com; Mexican; $$. At this small, family-friendly restaurant you feel like if you just listened hard enough you'd hear the waves outside the door. Large garage-style glass doors are raised during warm weather leaving only screens for walls and an alfresco dining experience throughout the entire restaurant. Dig into complimentary fresh salsa and chips as soon as you're seated, but not before you've placed an order for a prickly pear margarita. This pink, icy, and full-of-fresh-lime-flavor drink is as delicious as it is potent. It may be the signature drink, but there are plenty of other cocktail options—and indulging in a cocktail at this place that feels so beachy is practically mandatory. The menu is packed with traditional Mexican fare, including tacos, burritos, and quesadillas, but there's an emphasis on seafood, which should be noted. Start with the ceviche made with fresh fish in lime and orange juices with tomatoes, red onion, celery, and cilantro, or the crab fritters served alongside an avocado mayo and a sweet and sour chili sauce. Your main focus should be a few of Pure's fish tacos. These battered and fried white-fish tacos are served three to a plate and topped with fresh poblano slaw, creamy chipotle aioli, and tomatillo sauce. Olé!

Santé, 165 N. Trade St., Matthews, NC 28105; (704) 845-1899; santeofmatthews.com; American/French; $$$. Set in a building that's on the National Register of Historic Places, this downtown Matthews restaurant features exposed brick walls, an intimate year-round patio, a full bar, and beautiful paintings dotting the space. Named for the French phrase *"a votre santé,"* meaning to toast to your health, the restaurant is designed as a spot for cozy meals and celebratory gatherings. The dishes have a distinctly French leaning with appetizers like an Alsatian onion tart made with blue cheese and bacon crumbles or a truffle pate with fig jam and olive bread crostini. One of the menu's most beautifully presented dishes (the French would be proud) is actually a salad. The braised red cabbage salad is topped with the local Bosky Acres goat cheese, toasted pecans, and smoked bacon crisps, and drizzled in a flavorful balsamic vinaigrette. However, the entrees have plenty to offer as well. The chef focuses on using fresh, local, and often organic produce and the flavors shine through in entree selections like a braised lamb shank with a sweet potato puree, caramelized pearl onions, and lamb *jus* or the Springer Mountain Chicken Breast, stuffed with spinach, artichoke, and brie, and served over roasted-garlic whipped potatoes. While dinner may be the most popular hour at Sante's, lunch is a great time to enjoy the fruits of the chef in a more casual setting—and for lower prices. An extensive sandwich and wrap menu includes options like a grilled ham and brie sandwich with caramelized onions and a vegetarian hummus wrap made with spinach, roasted red peppers, avocado, sliced red onion, and chunks of feta cheese. Regardless of when you go, you can anticipate getting a taste of the flavor of the charming downtown Matthews with your visit.

Villa Antonio Italian Restaurant, 14825 John J. Delaney Dr., Ballantyne, Charlotte, NC 28277; (704) 369-5060; villaantonio.com; Italian; $$$. Like any really great Italian restaurant, you'll smell the garlic before you've hit the door of this Ballantyne spot. Whether you're looking for a romantic, candlelit dinner on the patio or just in search of some of the city's best Italian food, you've come to the right spot. The spacious Villa Antonio offers plenty of personality from an owner who is as likely to kiss your hand as shake it and live music featuring performances of singers from Sinatra to Elvis. For a bargain, stop by at lunch to enjoy the $10 lunch buffet, but for the full, Old World Italy experience, dinner is a must. You'll start with warm and fluffy focaccia bread alongside savory olive oil. An array of appetizers and salads are traditional Italian fare and while there are plenty of meat and seafood dishes, some of the best options can be found among the pastas. A decadent lobster ravioli features pillows of pasta stuffed with the tender shellfish in a house-made cognac cream sauce while a traditional lasagna made with seasoned beef, herbed ricotta, and mozzarella cheese is the kind of dish that will make you close your eyes and envision a Roman trattoria. In true gourmet Italian style, there are several veal offerings and Villa Antonio does these right. The veal piccata with its tender meat, lemon, capers, artichokes, and white wine may be the best in town. As your meal concludes you'll be given your choice from the dessert trolley. Options like cannoli and cheesecake are good, but your server will likely insist on the house-made tiramisu. Agreeing to that is an excellent choice.

Vintner Wine Market, 8128 Providence Rd., Charlotte, NC 28277; (704) 543-9909; vintnerwinemarketnc.com; Tapas; $$. From the outside you might guess that this was simply a wine store, but that would be a huge mistake. While there is an impressive selection of wines both by the bottle and the glass, the menu here could stand alone. When it comes to pairing with the vino, the cheese and charcuterie boards may be some of the best options. Featuring the chef's artisan cheese and cured meats selection, the boards are served with pairings like olives, plum compote, and whole-grain mustard. For a richer meal try the grilled cheese with beer-braised short ribs sandwich. Topped with spicy mustard and served with warm spiced chips, this is comfort food at its best. A selection of flatbreads and wings rounds out the eclectic menu— and knowledgeable servers with tips for wine pairing round out the experience. For a sweet finishing touch, order one of the naturally infused truffles created by the local Secret Chocolatier. While the selection changes daily, look for unusual and delicious flavors like Earl Grey and Mexican Cinnamon.

The Waldhorn Restaurant, 12101 Lancaster Hwy., Pineville, NC 28134; (704) 540-7047; waldhorn.us; German; $$. Pineville might not be where you'd expect to find a traditional German restaurant, but the Waldhorn restaurant is full of surprises. The owners, whose families are from Germany, opened the spot in June 1999. At lunchtime you'll find options like a grilled bratwurst sandwich topped with sauerkraut and served on a pretzel hoagie or a traditional wiener schnitzel served with french fries. Dinner, though, is the best time to dig into the authentic German fare—mostly because then you can really enjoy the pints of German beer alongside it. Try the Genbraten Ente, an oven-roasted half duck with an orange-apple sauce served with bread dumplings and red cabbage, or the *Rindsouladen,* a braised beef roulade stuffed with bacon, onions, and pickles and served with spaetzle and red cabbage. Try them alongside beers like the Warsteiner Pils or the Spaten Optimtor. There's no doubt this spot has the best German beer selection in the city, with more than 10 German brews on draft and additional options in bottles. If you're a German beer lover, join the club. For $29 you're given a half-liter stein mug filled with the draft of your choice. Then, each time you come back, you're given 50 cents off the regular draft price. And to really enjoy the beer selection here, head to Waldhorn for Oktoberfest when on Friday and Saturday through September and October, you can enjoy live German bands, dancing, beers, and food in the restaurant's large outdoor tent. Who needs Munich?

Landmarks

Jake's Good Eats, 12721 Albemarle Rd., Matthews, NC 28227; (704) 545-4741; jakesgoodeats.com; Southern; $. After being featured on the Food Network's popular *Diners, Drive-ins, and Dives,* this Southern comfort food spot began getting the attention it deserves. Located in a Gulf gas station from 1929, you'll find plenty of antique memorabilia on both the exterior and inside. While the restaurant itself has only been around since 2008, it feels as if it's been a local staple for years. Maybe that's the historic building and cozy character, but it could just be the down-home Southern cuisine. Items like fried green tomatoes and maple-glazed pork chips are the kind of thing you'll want to return for over and over again. Most of the menu is on the casual side with hot dogs, burgers, and a tasty BLT making the lunch menu. Dinner offers more upscale items like the grilled salmon brushed with honey mustard and molasses glaze over asparagus and mushroom risotto or the pan-seared New York Strip. But the best item on the menu may be Mrs. Sue's Seasonal Vegetable Plate, filled with savory, locally grown veggies piled high. And, if you're going to continue down the comfort food route, finish up your dinner with the creamy banana pudding. You'll be glad you did.

Specialty Stores, Markets & Producers

Dean & Deluca, 7804 Rea Rd., Stonecrest, Charlotte, NC 28277; (704) 541-7123; deandeluca.com. At this smaller version of the gourmet market located in SouthPark's Phillips Place, you'll find prepared foods and a small deli. You'll also find coffee and pastries in the morning, sandwiches and salads at midday, and elegant dishes to reheat at home in the evenings. While there's not much room for sitting in the shop, there is a small patio outside, perfect for enjoying a bite and a drink when you're in the neighborhood.

Matthews Farmers' Market, 188 N. Trade St., Matthews, NC 28105; matthewsfarmersmarket.com. Those in search of fresh, local produce can find it year-round at this community farmers' market that has been around for more than two decades. All of the products and food sold here are grown, raised, or made within 50 miles of the market, which means that you're getting some of the region's top offerings. From April to November, you'll find more than 50 vendors selling their wares, while from December through March, the number is closer to 25. All set in charming downtown Matthews, the market feels like a trip back to a simpler time. Plan your trip to the market on days when you can catch a glimpse of local chefs giving tips and teaching classes on producing top recipes and meals from seasonal fare. Plus many Saturdays you'll find live entertainment from local musicians and performers for enjoying while you shop.

The Meat House, 8410 Rea Rd., Charlotte, NC 28277; (704) 341-4276; themeathouse.com. This franchise may have locations across the country from New York to Texas to California, but its interior, stuffed with gourmet goods, gives the feeling of your neighborhood shop. Meat lovers in particular will love the selection of cuts like pork chips, filet, porterhouse, rib eye, and strip, but there's enough variety here to please any shopper. You'll find shelves filled with wines, olive oils, and gourmet sauces and rubs. Cases full of cheeses and veggie sides are also worth checking out. Plus you'll find prepared meats like stuffed chicken breasts, marinated ribs, or kabobs. Whether you're searching for a pre-prepared dinner or a place to inspire your cooking creativity, this stylish grocer has what you need.

West Charlotte

Belmont & Mount Holly

While many cities tend to expand horizontally, to the east and west, Charlotte has been different. Lake Norman to the north and Lake Wylie to the south, as well as a several other factors, meant that Charlotte grew taller rather than wider.

To the west of the city, you'll find several wide streets leading into town, most lined with strip malls and dotted with chain fast-food restaurants. However, go a little farther down I-85 and you'll come to small and charming town centers. Charlotte commuters live here, and the towns offer a chance to take a breath away from the business and bustle of the city.

Spots like Belmont are perfect for spending a comfortable day absorbing the small-town vibe as you peek into the General Store, walk along the historic main street, and grab a bite at the local fish camp. It's the kind of place where time moves a little slower—and when you're sipping on your sweet tea alongside your crispy fried catfish, you'll be glad that's the case.

Jax Backstreet Tavern, 55 Glenway St., Belmont, NC 28012; (704) 825-1776; jaxbackstreet.com; Pub; $$. Owned by the same folks behind the more upscale and nearby Old Stone Steakhouse, this easygoing tavern offers casual dishes like fried green beans with a blue-cheese horseradish dip, tater tots covered in chili, bacon, and cheese, and fried pickles alongside cool ranch sauce. These are the bites you might grab if you're dropping by to catch the game or spend an evening enjoying their draft and bottled beer selection—many of which are offered by the pitcher. But there are plenty of dishes for those in search of a decent midday meal or dinner. Salads, pizzas, sandwiches, wings, and tacos make up most of the menu and many weekend nights you'll find the spot brimming with people enjoying live music from local bands alongside their meal. Whatever you do, don't leave without ordering the deep-fried Snickers bar dessert. Outside of carnival season you're unlikely to find one of these around and this decadent treat is just as rich—and delicious—as you'd imagine.

Niko's Grill, 4948 Airport Center Pkwy., Charlotte, NC 28208; (704) 394-6520; American/Greek; $. You know the old adage that if there are police cars in front, the restaurant must be good? If that's how this small, off-the-beaten-path restaurant's level was measured, it would be known as the best spot in town. Seemingly always full of officers stopping in for a bite, the line is often out the door with those craving their chicken Parmesan sandwich, Philly cheesesteak, and gyros. It's a tucked-away, no-frills kind of place where you order at the counter and wait for your number to be called. But what it lacks in atmosphere it makes up for in hearty portions of great salads and sandwiches.

Old Stone Steakhouse, 23 South Main St., Belmont, NC 28012; (704) 825-9995; oldstonesteakhouse.com; Seafood/Steakhouse; $$$. Located in the center of Belmont's main street, this steakhouse has been a local favorite ever since a Charlotte restaurateur opened it several years ago. For the most part the menu is quintessential steakhouse fare from calamari and crab cake appetizers, to wedge salad, to steaks of all different sizes and cuts. Some of the menu's top sellers, though, aren't actually of the red meat variety. A full rack of baby back ribs are fall-off-the-bone tender and smothered in their signature Cheerwine barbecue sauce and a pork chop comes topped with a smoked bacon-apple glaze and drizzled with a lemon *beurre blanc*. With dishes like these you'll almost forget about the extensive steak selection. With its long side patio Old Stone is also a good spot to stop by for lunch when they serve up a variety of burgers including their famed Carolina Burger topped with savory chili and melted cheddar cheese. And don't be deterred from the patio based on weather. Throughout the winter, the area has enough heat lamps to ensure you can dine alfresco all year long.

Airport Eating

Forget the days of chain Chinese food or greasy burgers while waiting for that delayed flight. At **Charlotte Douglas Airport,** there are a few food choices that will make you cross your fingers your flight is running behind on your next trip.

For those in search of a taste of Carolina 'cue before leaving the state behind, stop in at the **Brookwood Farms BBQ** restaurant in the main atrium. The pulled-pork sandwiches are stuffed with the tender meat and the side selection is excellent, including mac and cheese, fried okra, broccoli casserole, and hush puppies. Plus every meal comes with a fried pickle spear, which means there's really little excuse for a visit to the Queen City without trying the region's favorite fried dish.

Also in the central atrium, you'll find the **First in Flight Bar,** a sleek, sophisticated bar in the very center of the airport. The bar itself is pleasant with seating offering some of the best people watching in the place, but it also offers **Hissho Sushi** (the airport's only sushi), which is remarkably good and a nice diversion from the typical fast food in airport terminals.

The best place to escape in the terminal is the **Carolina Beer Company,** which feels like a casual corner pub—not as if it's in the middle of the busy D Concourse. Sip on a pint of local brew and grab a sandwich before you hop on your flight.

The airport's newest culinary addition is **Bad Daddy's Burger Bar,** the city's favorite burger restaurant that also has locations in Dilworth and South Charlotte. If you have the time, grab a table and settle in for the restaurant's famed burgers, salads, tots, sweet potato fries, and a creamy milk shake to finish it all off. When they're serving the pretzels on the plane, you'll be glad you did.

River's Edge Bar and Grill, US National Whitewater Center, 5000 Whitewater Center Pkwy., Charlotte, NC 28214; (704) 391-3900; usnwc.org; American; $$. Prefer your sandwiches with a side of adventure? At the US National Whitewater Center, you can enjoy soups, salads, sandwiches, burritos, burgers, and entrees like pasta or salmon, all on a deck overlooking the rapids. From your seat you can watch rafters and kayakers paddling—and if you're lucky, for entertainment purposes, occasionally swimming—in the Class III and IV rapids with a cold, local brew in hand. The menu is varied, with a tasty selection of salads and several popular burgers, but for those just looking for a shared post-ride bite with their brews, this is an easy stop. Starters range from the gourmet seared tuna with avocado and field greens to the more casual sweet potato waffle fries served alongside honey mustard and jalapeño jelly. Watching rafters navigate the falls not enough entertainment for you? Check the website ahead of time for nights when you'll find live music entertainment and occasionally even fireworks, like the popular River Jam series throughout the summer.

Sammy's Pub, 25 South Main St., Belmont, NC 28012; (704) 825-4266; sammys belmont.com; Pub; $$. This casual pub has been serving Belmont since 1994 and the devoted clientele is evident as soon as you walk in. A large bar featuring multiple televisions and offering more than 60 beers is the restaurant's focal point. Tall windows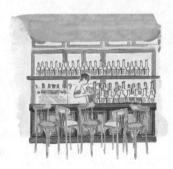

face the street from an interior filled with bar-top tables and stools scattered across hardwood floors, with booths lining one wall. You can dig into garden salads, burgers, sandwiches, and specialties like fish and chips or a rib eye dinner. Although, some of the more casual items like the fried dill pickles served with ranch dressing are favorites here. Of course, many of the most popular items are those served from behind the bar. A Bloody Mary offers a spicy kick and draft beers are served in frosted pint glasses. Settle in and plan on staying for awhile. This is the small-town kind of bar where you'll want to linger.

Landmarks

Bar-B-Q King, 2900 Wilkinson Blvd., Charlotte, NC 28208; (704) 399-8344; barbqking.com; Barbecue; $. For 50 years this casual barbecue joint has been serving up barbecue fried chicken, onion rings, coleslaw, chopped pork, hush puppies, seafood, and even po' boys. From the outside it looks as if Bar-B-Q King, with its red curbside service sign, is in a time warp from the 1960s. However, a few visits from the Food Network have breathed new life into the casual spot. In 2007 Guy Fieri showed up to feature it on *Diners, Drive-ins & Dives* and then in 2011 it was shown on *The Best Thing I Ever Ate*. These days the barbecue chicken, served with sides like potato salad or french fries (and, of course, with plenty of sweet tea), has become a practically mandatory meal for visiting foodies. Go on Thursday when you can get a quarter of a chicken with two sides and dinner rolls for $5.49. It may be the most delicious deal in town.

Catfish Cove, 1401 Armstrong Ford Rd., Belmont, NC 28012; (704) 825-3332; Seafood/Southern; $. Bring your cash and your appetite to this riverside fish camp because they don't take credit cards and you're going to want to be hungry when you're staring down heaping plates of their Southern fare. The home-style restaurant on the banks of the Catawba features offerings like fried chicken, meatloaf, mac and cheese, and, of course, fried fish. It's a casual, family-owned spot with a Sunday buffet that fills up fast with the after-church crowd. Skip the desserts and grab a piece of the penny candy from the register on your way out—it's the best way to round out the back-in-time experience of this country kitchen.

Neighbor's Brightstar Drive-In Grill, 201 Madora St., Mount Holly, NC 28120; (704) 827-0212; brightstargrill.com; Hamburgers; $. This 1950s throwback restaurant just down from the Belmont Drive-In Theater serves up some of the best burgers in the area. Black-and-white-tiled floors, casual booths, and red accents set the tone for the laid-back restaurant. A simple salad bar means those who prefer something a little less decadent than the piled-high burgers now have an option. But you'll still find plenty of serious Southern favorites here like fried bologna or pimento-cheese sandwiches. Plus, you'd be hard pressed to find better deals than the occasional specials here like six hot dogs for $6 one day or two mini burgers and fries for $5. Whatever you order, chances are it's a bargain—and it's tasty.

Specialty Stores, Markets & Producers

Belmont Farmers' Market, Main St. (across from the General Store), Belmont, NC 28012; facebook.com/Belmont-Farmers-Market. Located in a lot off Main Street just across from the General Store, this seasonal market sells all your local favorites. Spring and summer bring tables full of tomatoes, squash, okra, and peaches, all grown on nearby farms. Throughout the season you can find beef and pork products from nearby farmers, baked goods and roasted nuts from local vendors, and fresh-cut flowers from regional gardens. The market opens at 8 a.m. and continues until the goods are gone, so get there early to pick up the freshest and best produce.

The String Bean Fresh Market & Deli, 106 N. Main St., Belmont, NC 28102; (704) 825-3636; stringbeanmarket.com. At this charming deli you can sit down for a full meal of gourmet dishes like fried green tomatoes, warm brie and spinach salad, or fig and prosciutto flatbread. But many of the spot's best offerings come in its marketplace. A deli case features Boar's Head meats and cheeses as well as made to prepare items like creamy twice-baked potatoes, crab-stuffed mushrooms, deviled eggs, and stuffed tomatoes. You'll also find a large variety of wine and beer (more than 200 brews from around the world, many of which can be mixed and matched for their make-your-own six-packs), perfect for pairing with your newly purchased goods. Like what you find on the wine aisle? Check out one of their monthly wine- and beer-tasting events, where you can sample from their impressive selection.

Cocktail Culture

Whether you're searching for the city's sleekest wine bar or a place where you can pull a stool up to the bar and settle in for a good beer and an even better story, Charlotte has plenty of options. From neighborhood pubs and breweries to uptown cocktail lounges, consider this your exclusive guide to the city after dark.

Wine Bars

Dean & Deluca Wine Room, 6903 Phillips Place Ct., SouthPark, Charlotte, NC 28210; (704) 643-6868; deandeluca.com. If there was ever a place to see and be seen in Charlotte, it's the patio of this upscale SouthPark wine bar nestled among the upscale shops of Phillips Place. You'll find more than 70 wines by the glass, as well as wine flights with three varieties of wine and light tapas like cheese plates for nibbling. Whether you're stopping in before a movie at the center's cinema or settling in for an afternoon of indulging, it's a relaxing spot to soak up South Charlotte's stylish vibe. And while there is a luxurious interior with high ceilings and large windows, the sidewalk patio is the main draw here, where you can enjoy your glass while you watch the scene at the city's swankiest shopping center.

Dolce Vita Wine Bar, 3205 N. Davidson St., NoDa, Charlotte, NC 28205; (704) 334-1052; dolcevitawines.com. This is a wine bar for those people who prefer their drink to come with convivial conversation, a touch of live music, and an overstuffed couch. It's casual and easygoing with windows that open onto the street in warmer weather and a soundtrack that is indie and often local. You can order wines by the glass off the menu, or just snag a bottle from a shelf and wait for a server with glasses to open it up. The menu is simple, with a few sandwiches, pizzas, and bites, but the baked brie with a balsamic and honey glaze is the perfect creamy and rich appetizer for sharing while you sip. If you're hoping to include this as a stop on a weekend night, come early to grab a seat—especially if it's on the evening of one of the neighborhood's popular and always-busy gallery crawls.

D'Vine Wine Cafe, 14815 Ballantyne Village Way, Ballantyne, Charlotte, NC 28277; (704) 369-5050; dvinewinecafe.com. The wine shop part of this cafe is massive, with more than 600 different varieties, but the cafe is casual and relaxed with 35 wines by the glass and a variety of craft beers. The menu is more extensive than most wine cafes, with dishes like a seafood fettucine featuring shrimp and scallops tossed in a white-wine sauce or a filet with a wild mushroom and shallot ragout. The outdoor balcony area is a perfect stop for a summer night, with over-stuffed sofas and often live music. Whatever season you choose to go, keep an eye out for the cafe's quarterly Saturday afternoon tastings in which you can taste more than 20 different wines.

Press Wine and Food, 333 W. Trade St., Uptown, Charlotte, NC 28202; (704) 370-3006; presswinefood.com; $$. This cozy wine bar is all about the vino and with more than 100 bottles of wine, all priced at retail price, you'll want to settle in for a nice long sip. Not sure what you're in the mood for? Ask one of the knowledge-able servers. They'll direct you to the best bottles for pairing with your fare—or for simply enjoying on its own. There are overstuffed couches—and even board games—as well as casual cafe tables for enjoying small plates like sushi or paninis, but the best seat here is on the patio where you can soak in skyline views while you enjoy your red or white.

Urban Sip, 201 E. Trade St., Uptown, Charlotte, NC 28202; (704) 547-2244; ritzcarlton.com; $$. Located on the 15th floor of the

Ritz-Carlton, this wine and scotch bar has the feel of an upscale hotel lounge, but offers much more impressive views. The menu is designed for wine pairing with small plates, charcuterie, and cheeses. Dishes like steak tartare with poached quail egg, smoked cheddar fritters with a raspberry cabernet dipping sauce, or ahi tuna tacos are perfect for pairing with a drink. Can't decide on one wine? Not a problem. Urban Sip offers 10 different flights ranging from simple reds to elegant Champagne. A nice touch on the menu is the focus on local, including many of the cheeses and even going so far as having many of the dishes incorporate honey from the hotel's rooftop beehives. Or, if you'd prefer to drink your honey, try the Rooftop Honey Brandy Sour, their cocktail that incorporates the sweet treat.

The Wooden Vine, 231 N. Tryon St., Uptown, Charlotte, NC 28202; (704) 376-8463; thewoodenvine.com. With its gleaming hardwood floors, dark leather seating, and casual oak tables, this Uptown spot feels cozy before you've even settled in with a glass of red or white. The lunch menu includes larger items like shrimp and grits with a slow-poached fried egg and local Cloister honey or mussels drenched in a white-wine broth. But the kitchen's talent for creating perfect pairings for wine really shines on the evening tapas menu, which offers traditional Spanish treats like braised chorizo and perfectly crisp potatoes served alongside charred tomato aioli. There are more than 40 white varieties, and 60 red, with 30 wines by the glass. And if you prefer brews to vino, they've even got a few craft beers for drinking alongside your tapas.

Breweries

Ass Clown Brewing Company, 27039 Kenton Dr., Cornelius, NC 28301; (704) 995-7767; assclownbrewery.com. The name is, well, amusing. And the motto that goes along with it, "Don't be one, drink one!" is also entertaining. As you can imagine there's plenty of popular gear other than beer sold in this Cornelius brewery. There are, however, 12 different drafts in their taproom, which can be enjoyed in their tasting room by appointment on weekdays. Year-round you'll find their Apricot Seed Pale Ale, an Orange Spice IPA, a Dark Chocolate Blueberry Porter, a Vanilla Bean Chocolate Brown Ale, and an India Pale Ale. Seasonally beer lovers can enjoy plenty of other sweet-themed choices like the dark-chocolate pumpkin porter, a perfect brew for a chilly fall night.

Four Friends Brewing, 10913 C Office Park Dr., 28273; (704) 233-7071; fourfriendsbrewing.com. As you probably guessed this brewery was started by four friends, who, incidentally, had the idea over a few beers. You'll find their beers at plenty of favorite Charlotte restaurants like **Cabo Fish Taco** (p. 98) in NoDa or Uptown's

Dandelion Market (p. 28), or you can visit their tasting room in east Charlotte. Their top-selling Queen City Blonde and Queen City Red are always available and the brewery frequently offers limited releases like Gold Rush, an easy-drinking Belgian Style Blonde.

NoDa Brewing Company, 2229 N. Davidson St., NoDa, Charlotte, NC 28205; (704) 451-1394; nodabrewing.com. Get the Coco Loco Porter. Seriously. Don't skip this beer. There's a light chocolate flavor with a hint of toasted organic coconut that creates a mildly sweet flavor perfect for indulging in by the pint. There's a reason this beer has taken home prizes from a variety of competitions. You'll find a variety of other creatively named beers at this NoDa brewery, like Monk's Trunks, a Belgian pale ale with fruity flavors and Ramble on Red, a red ale with rye malt. The tap room is open most evenings until 8 p.m. and if you're lucky you'll catch the friendly and helpful Owners, Todd and Suzie Ford, while you're there. Or you can always find these beers at spots like **The Pizza Peel & Tap Room** (p. 164) in Cotswold and even **Basil Thai Restaurant** (p. 23) uptown.

The Olde Mecklenburg Brewery, 215 Southside Dr., South End, Charlotte, NC 28217; (704) 525-5644; oldmeckbrew.com. This South Charlotte brewery has been around since 2008 and you can find their beers at more than 200 bars and restaurants around Charlotte and into South Carolina. The tap room is open every day except Monday, but Saturday is the best day for visiting when free tours of the 30,000-square-foot brewery are offered at 2 p.m., 3 p.m., and 4 p.m. There are a variety of seasonal offerings as well as

Live Music, Good Food

Whether you prefer your barbecue with a side of blues or to enjoy jazz tunes while you dig into a steak, Charlotte offers plenty of spots to watch, listen, and eat simultaneously. As you might expect in a Southern city, some of the best music comes from local talent strumming away and crooning country tunes at spots serving up dishes like pimento cheese or barbecue ribs. One of the most well-known places in town to find live bands alongside good food is **Mac's Speed Shop** (2511 South Blvd., South End, Charlotte, NC 28203; 704-522-6227; macspeedshop.com) in South End, where the front patio overflows into the parking lot many nights as everyone from bikers to bankers piles in for one of the restaurant's famed chopped 'cue sandwiches and music from local bands.

If you're more in the mood for jazz and a swanky evening out, a spot like **Blue Restaurant & Bar** (206 N. College St., Uptown, Charlotte, NC 28202; 704-344-9222; bluecharlotte.com) in Uptown

several constants, but the OMB Copper, their flagship beer, and an authentic Dusseldorf-style Altbier, remain the top sellers. Settle in post-tour to try one for yourself in their tap room or in the sunny outdoor *biergarten*.

Skull Coast Ales, 802 Somerton Dr., Fort Mill, SC, 29715; (803) 619-9295; skullcoastbrewing.com. Ahoy, matey! These ales, brewed just over the border in South Carolina, have quickly become a cult is perfect for catching new acts every night while you dine on dishes like seared *foie gras* or sip one of their signature martinis. **Sullivan's Steakhouse** (1928 South Blvd., South End, Charlotte, NC 28203; 704-335-8228; sullivanssteakhouse.com) in South End frequently hosts jazz musicians as well and patrons can take them in while noshing on a filet or fresh seafood dish.

Not sure what you want? Head to NoDa, the funky neighborhood just east of town where music reigns. Here you can listen to live sounds throughout the neighborhood while you're enjoying a slice at **Revolution Pizza & Ale House** (3228 N. Davidson St., NoDa, Charlotte, NC 28205; 704-333-4440; revolutionpizza.com) or while you're sipping coffee at **Smelly Cat Coffeehouse** (514 E. 36th St., NoDa, Charlotte, NC 28205; 704-374-9656; smellycatcoffee.com). And if you can't get enough over dinner, stop in at The Evening Muse or The Neighborhood Theater, where you'll find talented musicians almost any night of the week.

favorite in the Charlotte beer scene. Maybe it's fun flavors like the Sea Witch Watermelon Wheat Ale that uses real watermelons in its brew, or maybe it's rich tastes like the Gallows Point Dead Man's Porter that offers decadent hints of the chocolate and macadamia nuts found in its recipe. Regardless, these beers, which you can find in their pirate-friendly tap room, are a local treasure. Interested in learning how to make your own at home? Skull Coast has plans to launch the Southeast's first brewing school for home brewers hoping to move out of the garage and into a brewery.

Pubs & Taverns

The Flying Saucer, 9605 N. Tryon St., University, Charlotte, NC 28262; (704) 717-8179; beerknurd.com. Until recent years if you were a beer lover in Charlotte, this University area bar was your only hope for finding a variety that went beyond your typical domestics and imports. With more than 240 beers and more than 100 different brewing styles, it remains a top spot for those in search of a good brew. With plenty of televisions in a cozy setting, this is the ideal bar for beer nerds in search of a great brew with the game. The menu is your basic bar food with soft pretzels and dips being the top sellers. Looking for a specific beer? Check the bar's website, where you'll find the newest available on tap as well as an exhaustive listings of their choices, complete with explanations and descriptions of each brew.

Growler's Pourhouse, 3120 N. Davidson St., NoDa, Charlotte, NC 28205; (704) 910-6566; growlerspourhouse.com. Come on the weekends—or game night—and you'll be hard pressed to find a stool in this cozy NoDa pub. Owned by the same folks who run Crepe Cellar next door (and sharing their kitchen), Growler's is devoted to its craft beer. Beer lovers will find a constantly rotating selection of craft brews like Bell's, Smuttynose, and Bear Republic, as well as a menu dedicated to the best pairings for beer. This means you can dig into a house-ground sausage dog and potato chips or a doughy pretzel with house-made spicy mustard while you're enjoying a frosty pint. Or, for a real culinary treat, order up the popular Growler's Pourhouse Reuben. Topped with gruyère cheese, homemade sauerkraut, and house-made sriracha-based dressing, the sandwich is piled high with local corned beef and served alongside house-made chips. Your beer just met its best friend.

The Liberty, 1812 South Blvd., South End, Charlotte, NC 28203; (704) 332-8830; thelibertycharlotte.com. One step inside this South End gastropub and it's obvious you're in a place that loves its beer as much as its accompanying fare. Walls in the bar area feature row after row of classic, vintage beer ads, while the dining room walls are panels of blown-up images of bubbling beer. Run by two Charlotte restaurant veterans, the food here is creative and big on flavor. House-made pickles and soft pretzels are perfect for sharing, and tender pork belly sliders feature a creamy vanilla-bean sauce, making them both sweet and smoky. The menu changes frequently, but if you have the chance, visit when they're serving the Gasto-Pig, roasted pork alongside delicate crepes, crumbled peanuts, pickled pineapple, jalapeño peppers, and lettuce. It's an unexpectedly delicious dish.

Solstice Tavern, 3221 N. Davidson St., NoDa, Charlotte, NC 28205; (704) 342-2556; solsticetavern.com. Much of the draw to this neighborhood tavern is its wide, tree-shaded back deck where you'll find patio tables and television many nights, but is often filled with groups playing games like corn hole. The menu is fairly typical bar food, with plenty of shareable dishes like baskets of onion rings, chili and cheese fries, and even fried green beans. The burgers aren't bad and the sandwiches are a nice accompaniment for one of the bar's beers, wines, or mixed drinks. Tuesday nights feature popular trivia games, while other evenings offer weekly drink specials ranging from $12 Bud Light buckets on casual Sunday evenings to $5 Jager Bombs on the crowded Saturday nights.

Whiskey Warehouse, 1221 The Plaza, Plaza Midwood, Charlotte, NC 28205; (704) 334-7005; whiskeycharlotte.com. When this Plaza Midwood restaurant added its rooftop bar, it quickly became the top neighborhood destination for drinks with skyline views. However it had been a popular spot ever since its opening. After all not only does it offer dishes like ribs and wings, but you'll also find more than 60 different whiskeys and more than 50 different beers. With hardwood floors, exposed brick walls, and high-beamed ceilings, it's the kind of place that feels cozy even though it's fairly large. If you're coming on the weekend, get there early to nab a table—and expect a DJ downstairs. Or if you're looking for a place to watch the game, get there even earlier to grab a seat on one of the overstuffed leather couches in a small sitting area featuring its own flat-screen televisions.

World of Beer, 222 E. Bland St., South End, Charlotte, NC 28203; (704) 333-2080; southend.wobusa.com. Tucked on the ground floor of a South End condo complex close to the Bland Street light-rail stop, this Florida-based beer superstore offers more than 500 beers. Inside you'll find high- and low-top tables, plenty of televisions, and a casual bar where you can order one of the 60 rotating draft brews. While the bar doesn't offer food (there's no kitchen here), beer lovers can feel free to bring in their own fare from nearby restaurants like sandwich and bagel shops. If you can snag a table, some of the best are on the shop's patio where on Thursday, Friday, and Saturday nights you'll find live music. The best time to visit, though, may be for one of the spot's brewery nights. These nights are focused on specific brewers like Atlanta's Sweetwater Brewing Company and fill up fast with local beer nerds.

Cocktail Lounges

Apostrophe Lounge, 1400 S. Tryon St., South End, Charlotte, NC 28203; (704) 371-7079; apostrophelounge.com. South End's nightlife is an eclectic mishmash of live music venues, taverns, and spots like Apostrophe where you can chat over premium martinis with names like Such a Tease or On the Kitchen Counter. The crowd and music here reflect the neighborhood's mix, which means some nights you'll be clinking wine glasses at an after-work social while hip-hop beats are remixed for the dance floor, and on others the bar will be packed with an after-concert crowd. Regardless of when you go, the crowd is typically fashionable and indulging in the lounge's extensive drink menu. Expect a line on many weekend nights—especially post concert at one of the nearby music venues.

Cosmos Cafe, 300 N. College St., Uptown, Charlotte, NC 28202; (704) 372-3553; cosmoscafe.com. This Uptown cafe has been a favorite for years, and now its sister location in Ballantyne has become one of the 'burbs' top spots for drinks and dancing on the weekends. If you're there with dinner in mind, the upstairs dining loft is the perfect spot to enjoy the sushi or tapas menu while taking in views of the rest of the restaurant and the busy city street outside. But if you're there for the martinis or for one of the restaurant's famed drink special nights, you'll want to mingle in the Thirsty Camel Lounge, where you can sip on drinks like The Queen Charlotte, a tart drink made with Bombay, Campari, orange juice, Prosecco, and beach bitters— served with a slice of orange.

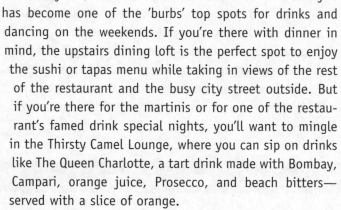

Crave Dessert Bar, 500 West 5th St., Uptown, Charlotte, NC 28202; (704) 335-0588; cravedessertbar.com. This may be the best place in Charlotte to end an evening in Uptown. Its exposed brick walls, dim lighting, soft thwomping house music, and lounge seating give it a sexy, urban feel that is reflected in its cocktail menu with drinks like Third Base, a sweet drink made with watermelon vodka and strawberry puree. But if you're at Crave, you should be ordering something with chocolate, whether it's The Victoria, three layers of rich chocolate cake with a chocolate buttercream icing, or the Chocolate Cocaine drink, a decadent mix of vanilla vodka and chocolate liqueur. Crave is open until 2 a.m. most nights, which means you can fulfill your cravings for things like dark-chocolate brownie cupcakes, double-decker strawberry shortcakes, or caramel pecan turtle cheesecakes until late in the evening. In the mood for hookah? This basement bar is one of the few spots in town where you'll find the flavor-filled pipes. Sweet, smoky choices like blueberry and strawberry may actually be the best pairings being served with those martinis.

Dive Bars

Jeff's Bucket Shop, 1601 Montford Dr., Charlotte, NC 28209; (704) 525-0425. Bars don't get much more casual—or beloved—than this hole-in-the-wall spot on Montford Drive. The street is buzzing on the weekends with young crowds of partiers out for the night at bigger bars like Andrew Blair's or **Brazwell's** (p. 167), but by the end of the evening, few are as tightly packed as this basement spot.

Just getting into Jeff's is an adventure as it's located in an old strip mall at the bottom of a narrow staircase below a giant neon arrow. Inside you'll find a small bar and an even smaller stage where most nights amusing karaoke goes on for hours. The surest sign this bar won't go out of style any time soon? In 2011 Jeff's lost its liquor license and never missed a beat as patrons brought their own drinks and paid corkage fees—all to hang out in this low-key bar.

Phil's Tavern, 105 East 5th St., Uptown, Charlotte, NC 28202; (704) 347-0035. Just off Tryon Street, Phil's is located around the block from some of the city's hottest nightlife. But this small, dimly lit tavern offers a certain low-key charm you won't find at the bigger spots. There's food if you're interested, including a decent bacon cheeseburger, but the main draw at Phil's Tavern in the evenings are the drinks and tiny dance floor, which gets packed on the weekends as a DJ spins top-40 mixes. Your best bet here will be to grab a stool, order a beer, and watch the lively crowds, which typically spill in from other bars late in the evening.

The Sanctuary, 507 East 36th St., NoDa, Charlotte, NC 28205; (704) 331-9797. If ever a neighborhood was made for a dive bar, it was the artsy and eclectic NoDa. Located next to the area's top attraction, Neighborhood Theater, this small spot fills with crowds on the night of a popular show and during the neighborhood's busy gallery crawls. Drinking (PBR is a favorite here) and people watching are the best reasons to come, but you'll also find pool tables, video games, and a jukebox to keep you entertained. Plus the food here, which is served until late in the evening, comes from Boudreaux's Louisiana Kitchen next door so *laissez les bon temps rouler* and dig into the gator bites while you soak up the scene.

The Thirsty Beaver, 1225 Central Ave., Plaza Midwood, Charlotte, NC 28204; (704) 332-3612. There are bras hanging from horns over the door, a Burt Reynolds poster in the corner, and a free vintage jukebox. As you might imagine from a small bar next to the railroad tracks, this spot is mostly locals—and draws lots of bikers, especially on nights with live music. Don't come here looking for a fancy mixed drink (unless it's one of their famously spicy Bloody Mary's) or a DJ spinning tunes (the music is mostly classic country with some Bob Dylan and Bruce Springsteen making the list as well). But if you're in the mood for a cold beer and conversation with laid-back folks, this is your place. And don't worry—you shouldn't have any trouble finding this one. Just look for the cowboy hat–wearing beaver painted on the side of an orange, cement block building.

Tommy's Pub, 2007 Central Ave., Plaza Midwood, Charlotte, NC 28205; (704) 377-0022. NASCAR fans should consider this bar a mandatory stop on a trip to town. Racing memorabilia and politically incorrect bumper stickers cover the walls, which have soaked up enough cigarette smoke over the years to make the dark bar constantly smell faintly of smoke and whiskey. The bartenders love to talk NASCAR so pull up a seat on one of the cracked vinyl bar stools and get ready for some good tales—which may or may not actually be true. While any night the music selection will likely be classic tunes from artists like Johnny Cash, the best time for music lovers to come may be on Tuesday, which is vinyl night. Bring your own collection and they'll play them for you while you chat with the old timers.

Recipes

Butterscotch Scones

Pewter Rose Bistro's Executive Chef Brent Martin has baked literally thousands of these golden scones. After all, they're complimentary to every diner who walks through the door at the charming South End restaurant during its popular brunch and breakfast. Occasionally the restaurant will offer a special version featuring chocolate chips or even coconut, but it's the original that is beloved by its frequent return visitors. Want to up the flavor? Increase the butterscotch count. You'll get an extra kick of sweet, melted goodness in every pastry.

Yields 12 scones

1 ¾ cups all-purpose flour

1 tablespoon plus 1 teaspoon baking powder

½ teaspoon kosher salt

1 large egg

⅓ to ½ cup whole milk

4 tablespoons unsalted butter, frozen

⅓ cup butterscotch chips

Heat oven to 375°F. In a bowl combine flour, baking soda, and salt. In a measuring cup with ounce markings, lightly beat egg and add milk to total 5 ounces.

Finely chop frozen butter. Cut butter into flour mixture using a fork. When the mixture resembles bread crumbs, add milk mixture, reserving 1 teaspoon of milk mixture. Stir gently to combine. Add butterscotch chips and stir gently, working the dough as little as possible.

Turn dough onto a lightly floured surface and fold it a few times. Using a rolling pin roll dough about 1 inch thick. Cut into 2-inch triangles. Transfer scones to an ungreased cookie sheet. Brush top of each scone with reserved milk mixture. Bake until lightly browned, 10 to 11 minutes. Serve while still warm.

Courtesy of Owner Susie Peck and Executive Chef Brent Martin of Pewter Rose Bistro (p. 74).

Banana Bread French Toast

While SouthPark's Terrace Cafe offers plenty of tasty lunch and dinner options, its breakfasts have quickly become some of the city's favorites. And with dishes like Executive Chef Thomas Kerns's sweet Banana Bread French Toast, it's easy to see why. This dish features several different components that may take some time to make. However, if you think you'll be in a hurry in the morning, create the bread and the syrup the night before. Then in the morning, the french toast won't take much longer than it does for your coffee to finish brewing.

Yields 6 servings

Banana Bread

2 cups (245 grams) all-purpose flour

¾ cup (150 grams) granulated sugar

¼ cup baking powder

1 pinch baking soda

1 pinch salt

1 teaspoon ground cinnamon

2 large eggs

2½ cups unsalted butter, melted and cooled

3 large bananas (approximately 1 pound or 454 grams)

1½ teaspoons vanilla extract

1 cup pecans

Preheat oven to 350°F. Butter and flour (or spray with nonstick cooking spray) loaf pan. In a large bowl combine flour, sugar, baking powder, baking soda, salt, and cinnamon. Set aside.

In a medium-size bowl combine the eggs, melted butter, mashed bananas, and vanilla. With a rubber spatula or wooden spoon, lightly fold the wet ingredients into the dry ingredients just until combined and the batter is thick and chunky. Scrape batter into prepared pan. Bake until bread is golden brown and toothpick *comes out clean, about 55–60 minutes. Place on wire rack to cool and then remove bread from pan.*

French Toast Batter

8 eggs

1 teaspoon vanilla extract

2 teaspoons ground cinnamon

½ teaspoon ground cloves

¼ teaspoon ground nutmeg

1 tablespoon sugar

½ cup whole milk

Whisk the eggs, vanilla, cinnamon, cloves, nutmeg, sugar, and milk together in a bowl; beat until fully incorporated.

Soak cool slices of banana bread in french toast batter. Grill until fully cooked.

Maple Rum Sauce

1 cup maple syrup

1 teaspoon almond extract

1 teaspoon vanilla extract

¼ ounce Bacardi rum

1 banana, sliced

¼ cup pecans, chopped

Combine Maple Rum Sauce ingredients in medium bowl and stir until fully mixed. Pour over french toast.

Courtesy of Executive Chef Thomas Kerns of Terrace Cafe (p. 170).

Crab Cakes with Pecan Remoulade

Chef Scott Hollingsworth has been turning out tasty dishes from Dressler's Restaurant kitchen since 2005. Some of his best dishes, which can be found at both the Lake Norman location and the location in the Metropolitan complex in Midtown, incorporate seafood. These tender crab cakes, brimming with fresh crab meat, are no exception. And while the cakes themselves could stand alone with their rich flavor, the pecan remoulade adds a Southern twist that will tempt you to lick your plate when you're finished. Lucky for you, now you can make the dish at home, where plate licking is much more acceptable behavior.

Yields 8 servings

Crab Cakes

2½ pounds crabmeat

3 eggs

1 tablespoon Old Bay seasoning

⅛ cup dijon mustard

2 tablespoons lemon juice

1 tablespoon Worcestershire sauce

1 tablespoon chopped parsley

1 cup mayonnaise

1 small bunch green onions, chopped

½ cup Japanese bread crumbs

Mix all ingredients well, trying not to break up the crabmeat too much. Shape into 8 patties. Heat oil in a large skillet over medium heat and carefully place crab cakes into pan to fry until brown (approximately 4 to 5 minutes). Fry on both sides and serve warm with remoulade sauce.

Pecan Remoulade

2 cups pecans

1 medium onion, finely diced

1 ounce butter

1 tablespoon Cajun seasoning

½ bottle Grey Poupon

1 tablespoon Worcestershire sauce

½ cup honey

4 cups mayonnaise

Toast pecans for 4 minutes at 350°F. Sauté onion in butter until tender and slightly browned. In mixing bowl combine pecans, onion, and all other ingredients (Cajun seasoning through mayonnaise).

Refrigerate in covered container before serving with crab cakes.

Courtesy of Owner Jon Dressler and Executive Chef Scott Hollingsworth
of Dressler's Restaurant (p. 120).

French Onion Soup

Gallery Restaurant may be located in a suburban American resort, but its French Onion Soup is worthy of a quaint Parisian bistro. The hearty soup is thick with soft, fresh onions and hints of port wine, while an herb focaccia bread crostina topped with Guinness beer–soaked gruyère cheese adds a rich flavor and texture. This soup can be enjoyed year-round, but it's perfect for warming up on a chilly night.

Yields 4 servings

- 4 medium yellow onions, thinly sliced
- 2 tablespoons canola oil
- 1 cup port wine
- 2 cups sherry wine
- 2 quarts beef stock
- Kosher salt
- Black pepper
- Herb focaccia bread
- Mozzarella, shredded
- Guinness beer–soaked gruyère cheese, shredded

In a heavy-bottomed pot, caramelize the onions in the oil very slowly over low heat to achieve a deep golden-brown color. The volume of onions will drop by at least half. Once the onions are sticky and dark brown but not burnt, add the port and sherry wines. Increase the heat to high and reduce until almost dry. Add the beef stock and simmer for 10 to 12 minutes. Season to taste with salt and black pepper.

For the crostini cut the focaccia to a size that will fit just inside the rim on the container in which you will be serving the soup.

To serve: Heat the soup, toast the bread, float the shaped crostini on the soup, cover the top of the crostini with a generous portion of both cheeses, and brown the whole thing under a broiler.

Courtesy of Chef de Cuisine J. Kelly Morrow of Gallery Restaurant (p. 197).

Chicken Tortilla Soup

When local restaurateur Frank Scibelli announced that he'd be opening Paco's Tacos & Tequila in the summer of 2010, Charlotteans rejoiced. After all this is the man behind spots like Mama Ricotta's, Bad Daddy's Burger Bar, and Cantina 1511. It seems that all he touches turns to culinary gold. Of course when he announced that he would be consulting on the restaurant's dishes with famed Tex-Mex culinary expert and cookbook author Robb Walsh, well, that's when Charlotte foodies went wild. The restaurant's menu is brimming with authentic Tex-Mex fare you'll want to dig into before washing it down with one of the restaurant's signature margaritas. While this soup is on the lighter side of many of the menu's offerings, it's perfect for making at home to give your night a taste of Tex-Mex.

Yields 8 servings

2½ teaspoons corn oil

2 teaspoons unsalted butter

1⅓ tablespoons minced and peeled garlic

½ cup small-diced white onion

½ cup small-diced celery

½ cup small-diced carrot

2 teaspoons seeded and diced serrano pepper

1 bay leaf

½ tablespoon kosher salt

½ teaspoon ground black pepper

Pinch cumin

1 cup canned fire-roasted tomatoes

½ cup tomato juice

5⅓ cups chicken stock

½ cup medium-diced red potato

½ cup roasted corn

6 cups shredded oven-poached chicken

3 cups tortilla strips

8 sprigs fresh cilantro

1 lime, sliced into 8 sections

1 thinly sliced jalapeño

1 pitted, peeled, and sliced avocado

Melt the oil and butter in a large stockpot over medium heat. When the butter melts add the garlic, onion, celery, carrot, serrano pepper, and bay leaf.

Sweat off 10–15 minutes until the ingredients are soft and translucent. Add the salt, pepper, and cumin and cook 2 minutes.

Add the tomatoes and tomato juice and simmer for 15 minutes.

Add the chicken stock. When it comes to a boil, reduce the heat and simmer for 30 minutes.

Add the potatoes and corn and simmer for 15 minutes. When the potatoes are cooked, remove from heat.

Stir in the shredded chicken. To serve, spoon the soup into a bowl, top each bowl with a handful of tortilla strips, a sprig of cilantro, and a slice of lime, jalapeño, and avocado.

Courtesy of Owner Frank Scibelli of Paco's Tacos & Tequila (p. 161).

Sweet Potato Crepes

Chef Marc Jacksina's creativity in the kitchen has produced many tasty dishes for Uptown's sleek and sophisticated Halcyon, Flavors from the Earth. The restaurant frequently uses local and seasonal produce and this recipe is no exception. For the freshest—and tastiest—version, use locally raised eggs and North Carolina sweet potatoes, which can be found at area farmers' markets when they're in season.

Yields 12–14 servings

Ricotta

½ gallon whole milk

2 cups buttermilk

1 cup heavy cream

1 lemon, juiced

1 teaspoon sea salt

In a medium stockpot combine all ingredients for the ricotta and bring to 175°F over medium-high heat, stirring frequently. Once temperature is achieved, shut off heat and allow to rest for 10 minutes. Using a mesh strainer scoop the curds into 4 layers of cheesecloth. Do not squeeze, but rather tie to a faucet and allow to drain for about 1 hour.

Praline Sauce

¾ cup butter

1⅓ cups light brown sugar

1 cup heavy cream

2 tablespoons honey

½ cup powdered sugar

1 tablespoon bourbon

1 cup chopped, toasted pecans

To make the praline sauce, in a small, heavy saucepan, combine the butter, light brown sugar, heavy cream, and honey and mix until well combined. Bring to a boil and let cook 1 minute, stirring constantly. Remove from heat and whisk in powdered sugar and bourbon. Stir in toasted pecans. Set aside and let cool for about 20 to 25 minutes. Sauce will thicken as it cools.

Sweet Potato Filling

½ cup light brown sugar
1 teaspoon ground cinnamon
1 teaspoon ground nutmeg

2 North Carolina sweet potatoes (about 1¾ pounds), roasted and scraped from their skins

For the sweet potato filling, mix the light brown sugar with the cinnamon and nutmeg, then add the sweet potatoes and mix until well blended. Reserve.

Crepes

1 cup all-purpose flour (4 ounces)
Pinch kosher salt
1¼ cups milk

3 large farm eggs, lightly beaten
4 tablespoons butter, melted
1 tablespoon chopped chives
Nonstick cooking spray

To make the crepes combine the flour, salt, and milk together in a bowl and mix with a hand mixer until smooth. Add eggs, beating well. Stir in the melted butter and chives. Coat the bottom of an 8-inch nonstick skillet with nonstick spray and heat over medium heat until hot. Pour about ¼ cup crepe batter into the skillet, then immediately tilt pan to coat bottom evenly. Cook for approximately 1 minute or until the bottom is lightly browned. Flip and cook for about 15–20 seconds longer. Transfer to a platter and repeat with remaining batter, spraying skillet several more times. Place wax paper sheets in between the crepes to prevent sticking.

To assemble the crepes spread about 1 tablespoon of ricotta and ⅓ cup sweet potato filling in the center of each crepe. Roll up and place in an 11 x 15-inch glass pan. Continue until you use up all the ingredients. Place the dish in a 300°F oven for 10 minutes or until just warm. Alternatively you can heat the crepes one at a time in a microwave on low for approximately 30 seconds or until the crepes are warm.

To serve place one filled crepe on the plate and top with warm honey-praline sauce that has been stirred to evenly distribute pecans. Sauce should still be warm, but if it isn't, heat on low just until warm, not hot.

Courtesy of Executive Chef Marc Jacksina of Halcyon, Flavors from the Earth (p. 30).

Rigatoni Tossed with Italian Sausage

Bruce Moffett, the Chef and Owner at Barrington's Restaurant, has been serving some of the city's best fare since his cozy bistro opened in the fall of 2000. The restaurant has received plenty of national acclaim for its flavorful dishes with a comfort food twist, like this hearty pasta. The mixture of the savory sausage, spicy chili flakes, and sweet Marsala gives this a distinct flavor unlike any pasta dish you've likely tasted in the past.

Yields 2 servings

2 ounces extra virgin olive oil
6 ounces cooked, crumbled fennel sausage
½ teaspoon chili flakes
12 ounces sweet Marsala
4 ounces veal stock

8 ounces Pomi strained tomatoes
8 ounces heavy cream
2 ounces grated Parmesan
16 ounces cooked rigatoni
1 bunch parsley, finely chopped

Heat olive oil in a large sauté pan and lightly toast the sausage in the oil.

Add chili flakes and toast for just a second. Deglaze the pan with the Marsala and reduce until it starts to thicken. Next add veal stock and reduce to a syrup. Add Pomi tomatoes and reduce by half. Add cream and Parmesan and reduce sauce until it clings to the back of a spoon. Toss in rigatoni and cook until the pasta is hot and the sauce starts to cling to the ridges. Season with salt to taste and serve with some more grated Parmesan and finely chopped parsley.

Courtesy of Executive Chef and Owner Bruce Moffett of Barrington's Restaurant (p. 142).

Metropolitan Meatloaf

At a restaurant as cozy and homey as Fran's Filling Station, it only makes sense that one of the best dishes would be something as comforting and hearty as meatloaf. Owner Fran Scibelli's recipe creates the savory kind of meatloaf you'll want to serve the next time you're hosting a casual get-together with friends. Pair it with creamy mashed potatoes and a glass of your favorite red wine, and it's sure to be an instant hit.

Yields 1 or 2 loaves

- ¼ cup canola/olive oil blend
- ¼ cup finely minced garlic
- ⅓ cup chopped scallions
- ½ cup finely chopped green bell pepper
- ¾ cup finely chopped red bell pepper
- ¾ cup peeled, finely chopped celery
- 1¼ cup finely chopped onion (either red or yellow is fine)
- 1 loaf sourdough or hearty white bread, processed or grated into bread crumbs
- 1⅛ cup buttermilk or milk

- 4 ounces dijon mustard
- 8 ounces ketchup
- 1 teaspoon Worcestershire sauce
- 2 pounds ground chuck and 1½ pounds each ground pork and ground turkey
- 5 eggs
- 1½ tablespoons salt
- 2 teaspoons ground black pepper
- 2 teaspoons ground cumin
- 2 teaspoons dried thyme
- ½ cup chopped fresh parsley

Sauté veggies in oil until translucent. Allow to cool completely.

Place bread crumbs in a large bowl and add buttermilk or milk. Stir together until bread is soft and liquid absorbed. Stir in mustard, ketchup, and Worcestershire sauce.

Combine in large mixing bowl, bread/milk mixture, veggies, and meat, and work together gently with your hands. Much of the quality of the meatloaf depends on not being overworked and handled gently and as little as possible. Beat eggs separately, then add to meat mixture along with seasonings. Mix until thoroughly blended.

At this point I like to make a small patty and cook it at 375°F for 12–15 minutes or until it registers 165°F on a meat thermometer. Taste and adjust seasonings if needed. Place remaining meat mixture in 1 or 2 well-oiled loaf pans or shape free form on a parchment-lined baking sheet and cook for 40–50 minutes or until they register 165°. If loaves are getting too brown before they are sufficiently cooked, cover loosely with foil.

Meatloaf will cut best if cooled at least slightly before cutting. Serve with extra catsup or brown gravy as desired.

Courtesy of Executive Chef and Owner Fran Scibelli of Fran's Filling Station (p. 63).

Salted-Caramel Brownies

The salty edge to this sweet treat made with dark, rich chocolate has made this the local bakery's top seller. And, while a trip to the eclectic bakery—either in its original NoDa spot or in its Uptown location—is always an enjoyable experience, this is the kind of dish you'll want to make just to assuage your cravings. When it comes to this sweet, don't even think about cutting where you can. There's a good reason Amelie's using high-butterfat European butter in their brownies. It produces a luscious dish so creamy you'll be licking your fingers after every bite.

Yields 24 brownies

6 ounces unsweetened chocolate, chopped

¾ cup unsalted butter, cubed

2 cups granulated sugar

3 large eggs

1 cup unbleached all-purpose flour

1¾ cups salted-caramel glaze (see below; prepare glaze when brownies are cool)

Heat oven to 325°F. Grease a 9-by-13-inch pan with butter or cooking spray.

In the top of a double boiler over medium heat, melt chocolate and butter, being sure the water in the bottom of the double boiler does not touch the top pan. Stir chocolate and butter until completely melted. Then stir in sugar. Blend well. Remove from heat.

In a separate bowl lightly whisk eggs. Stir eggs into chocolate mixture. Then add flour, stirring until completely blended. Spread batter into prepared pan and bake for 30 minutes.

Completely cool brownies in pan. Pour caramel glaze over brownies and cool until caramel sets. Slice into bars, about 2 inches square.

Salted-Caramel Glaze

½ **cup heavy cream**
2 **cups granulated sugar**
½ **cup water**
¼ **cup unsalted butter, cubed**

2 **teaspoons fine sea salt**
2 **tablespoons powdered gelatin, combined with ¼ cup cold water**

In a small saucepan over low heat, warm heavy cream until hot, but not boiling. In a separate tall saucepan, combine sugar and water. Place over medium-high heat. Do not stir as sugar dissolves and mixture reaches a dark amber stage. Add the heated cream, butter, and salt. Stir gently until mixture is smooth and well combined. Remove from heat and add gelatin, stirring to combine. Use immediately.

Courtesy of Owner Lynn St. Laurent and Assistant
Pastry Chef Eric Stanton
of Amelie's French Bakery (p. 21).

Appendix A: Eateries by Cuisine

Appendix B: Dishes, Specialties & Specialty Food

Index